THE ART OF
ACTIVE
LISTENING

THE ART OF
ACTIVE
LISTENING

HOW PEOPLE AT WORK FEEL HEARD, VALUED, AND UNDERSTOOD

HEATHER R. YOUNGER

BK

Berrett–Koehler Publishers, Inc.

Berrett-Koehler Publishers, Inc.
1333 Broadway, Suite 1000
Oakland, CA 94612-1921
Tel: (510) 817-2277 | Fax: (510) 817-2278
www.bkconnection.com

ORDERING INFORMATION

Quantity sales. Special discounts are available on quantity purchases by corporations, associations, and others. For details, contact the "Special Sales Department" at the Berrett-Koehler address above.

Individual sales. Berrett-Koehler publications are available through most bookstores. They can also be ordered directly from Berrett-Koehler: Tel: (800) 929-2929; Fax: (802) 864-7626; www.bkconnection.com.

Orders for college textbook/course adoption use. Please contact Berrett-Koehler: Tel: (800) 929-2929; Fax: (802) 864-7626.

Distributed to the U.S. trade and internationally by Penguin Random House Publisher Services.

Berrett-Koehler and the BK logo are registered trademarks of Berrett-Koehler Publishers, Inc.

Printed in Canada

Berrett-Koehler books are printed on long-lasting acid-free paper. When it is available, we choose paper that has been manufactured by environmentally responsible processes. These may include using trees grown in sustainable forests, incorporating recycled paper, minimizing chlorine in bleaching, or recycling the energy produced at the paper mill.

Library of Congress Cataloging-in-Publication Data
Name: Younger, Heather R., author.
Title: The art of active listening : how people at work feel heard, valued,
    and understood / Heather R. Younger.
Description: First edition. | Oakland, CA : Berrett-Koehler Publishers, Inc.,
    [2023] | Includes bibliographical references and index.
Identifiers: LCCN 2022046625 (print) | LCCN 2022046626 (ebook) |
    ISBN 9781523003884 (paperback) | ISBN 9781523003891 (pdf) |
    ISBN 9781523003907 (epub) | ISBN 9781523003914 (audio)
Subjects: LCSH: Listening. | Attention. | Interpersonal relations.
Classification: LCC BF323.L5 Y68 2023 (print) | LCC BF323.L5 (ebook) |
    DDC 153.6/8—dc23/eng/20221212
LC record available at https://lccn.loc.gov/2022046625
LC ebook record available at https://lccn.loc.gov/2022046626

First Edition
30 29 28 27 26 25 24 23   10 9 8 7 6 5 4 3 2 1

Book production: Linda Jupiter Productions   *Edit:* Elissa Rabellino
Text design: Kim Scott, Bumpy Design   *Proofread:* Daniel Gall
Artwork: Property of Employee Fanatix, LLC   *Index:* Mary Ann Lieser
Cover design: Susan Malikowski, DesignLeaf Studio

• • •

To my brilliant children:

Thank you for teaching me to listen better,
challenging me when I fail to be fully present,
and smiling on me with adoration when I listen well.

I'm forever grateful for each of you!

CONTENTS

• • •

FOREWORD

• • •

I've had the pleasure of knowing and working with Heather Younger over the past several years. We met while she was finishing her terrific book *The Art of Caring Leadership* at the same time I was in the middle of writing *Trust & Inspire*. As we connected, we learned that we were both very aligned in what we were experiencing in our respective work with leaders and in where the world was headed from a leadership perspective. This alignment has been validated as we've both been invited to speak on similar themes at the same events for the same client. I was honored to be able to endorse that book then, and even more thrilled to provide a foreword for this tremendous book now.

The Art of Active Listening is a natural and much-needed follow-on to *The Art of Caring Leadership*. What I find makes Heather's voice particularly powerful is that she is a model of both what she writes about and the kind of leadership we need today. I've experienced firsthand her unmatched ability to listen as she's worked with and helped me behind the scenes and as we've recorded podcasts and shared the stage together. I'm always struck by her perceptiveness and her curiosity about the world and others.

My father was fond of saying, "What air is to the body, understanding is to the heart." For anyone who has experienced a moment of deep understanding—or the opposite of it—this metaphor rings powerfully true. Everyone wants to feel heard, valued, and understood. Everyone wants to know their opinions matter. Everyone wants to know they are important. And when people don't feel this way, it can be suffocating. This book elevates the conversation on listening at work—taking it from something that can often feel vague or soft and turning it into a learnable, replicable process that, when completed, enables us to understand others and helps those we work with to feel that they matter. Heather's "Cycle of Active Listening" not only is insightful and additive to the work already out there; it's immensely and immediately practical.

Without knowing it at the time, I encountered the Cycle of Active Listening during my early days as a leader. I'll never forget my experience of helping to guide my company through a merger with another company. Although both organizations brought great content, practices, and people to the table, there was a clear disconnect between us as we merged companies. However, I was initially unaware of the magnitude of this gap. The truth is, I thought that I understood, and that I was doing a good job of listening to the needs and concerns of people. I knew the importance of empathy. In fact, one of the core tenets of my father's teachings was to "seek to understand," so I made this a key practice of mine—always trying to listen to others with good intent in my heart. We even held meetings specifically designed for people to share their feedback and concerns. So, you can imagine why I was both surprised and confused when my actions were consistently met with doubt and uncertainty. People didn't fully trust me, even though I felt like I was trustworthy. Something was missing.

I'll never forget preparing to give a strategy presentation with my business unit several months into the merger. I was anxious, as I knew there were rumblings about how things were going. Skepticism and doubt seemed to permeate every conversation, every meeting, every initiative. Swallowing nervously, I stepped into the room and was met with hesitation.

The body language in the room was despondent. The energy was tense, palpable, and charged with suspicion. Although I had planned to discuss our business unit's strategy, it was clear that this wasn't what was needed. There was something people weren't saying, and I could feel it. I knew a different approach was needed. So, I took a risk and opened up a real conversation with complete transparency—addressing concerns (both spoken and unspoken) no matter how difficult or personal they were. People were shocked at first but quickly saw that I was sincere in my desire to hear them and turn things around. They began to offer feedback and suggestions.

Instead of becoming defensive or shutting down ideas I didn't agree with, I tried my best to listen with an open mind. I asked follow-up questions and asked for additional perspectives. Internally, I had to examine my own potential biases that might keep me from fully understanding a different point of view. I adopted a very useful mantra to help me begin to recognize my own biases: "The height of subjectivity is to think you're objective; the height of objectivity is to know you're subjective and to take steps to compensate for it."

At the end of the meeting, we reviewed what we had discussed and the commitments we had made along the way, along with the items we had put in the "parking lot" for further discussion later. Once everyone felt heard and understood, we were able to act—together. Active listening enabled us to move from my goals for the merger to our goals. We focused on delivering on every one of the commitments we had made in the meeting and taking on the issues we had put to the side. Over time, we worked together to create initiatives and put plans in place that would help the merger run more smoothly. We built in systems of accountability, so that we could follow up and report back on how plans were being executed effectively.

What was originally scheduled to be a one-hour presentation became a whole day of collaboration and months of follow-on action. People came in tired and left energized—including me. I could have just plowed ahead with the meeting and talked about strategy for an hour as planned. But it would have been ineffective and uninspiring. The underlying issues would have remained and prevented meaningful progress.

This book beautifully maps out and explains a process that I stumbled into. Although I didn't know it at the time, with that meeting and our follow-on actions over the next several months, I unwittingly went through each of Heather's five steps of her Cycle of Active Listening with my team. The result was that we communicated better, created sustainable changes, and bridged the divide that once stood in our way.

Reflecting on other experiences, I see the Cycle of Active Listening playing out naturally with many of the most effective leaders I've known. That's how you know the framework is valid—it shows up repeatedly in different situations, contexts, and relationships. Like me, I think you'll see your own successes in this book, and it will help you see missed opportunities and missteps with greater clarity.

I'm reminded of a leader I worked with who modeled the Cycle of Active Listening after receiving really difficult feedback in a 360-degree assessment. Many leaders tend to look at difficult feedback and discount it, simply assuming a lack of understanding on the part of the people giving it. Henry David Thoreau once said, "It's not what you look at that matters, it's what you see." She didn't want to just have the feedback, she really wanted to "see," to understand.

She thanked people for participating, shared what she had heard from the feedback, and then asked follow-up questions to get a deeper understanding. She examined her own biases and set them to the side as she tried to gain a clear picture of herself and her abilities. She worked to decode and to figure out the unsaid. Then she sprang into action, making an improvement plan based on the feedback and sharing it with her team. They were invited to help her improve and to help her be accountable. When the second survey came around, she scored far better than before, not only because she had improved but also because people felt that she had truly heard and understood what they had told her. Not just because she listened, but because she acted.

Like Heather, I'm not suggesting that every piece of feedback or advice you get needs to be implemented. Understanding does not equal agreement, and you might not always agree with what's being said, or there may be mitigating circumstances that keep you from implementing certain ideas. But when you disagree from a place of understanding, people feel heard and valued, even if you don't take their recommendation.

These experiences drive home what I believe is the true test of understanding. It is not when you are able to say to someone, "I understand you," but rather it is when that person is able to say to you, "I feel understood. Thank you for listening." Heather's Cycle of Active Listening—with each of its essential steps—is a path to deep understanding.

Never before has there been a greater need for more listening and understanding in our world than today! The more advanced we become, the more complex our problems, too. Access to unlimited and constant information is both a blessing and a curse—it can enlighten, but it can also consume. Listening in the digital age has presented new challenges—and not just because someone accidentally mutes themselves on Zoom. Listening at work today means more than just hearing words; it means understanding people, their background, their experiences, their context, their humanity.

There is more noise today than ever before. With all the platforms for electronic communication and social media and the like, talking has never been easier, and listening effectively has never been more difficult. Yet this is a crucial skill that is needed in every relationship, team, and organization. In order to achieve at the highest levels, in order to function as cohesive teams, in order to build strong bonds, we must be in the business of listening to and understanding one another at work. Getting good at this matters.

For all our progress and awareness of the importance and potential contained in active listening, it continues to be among our most persistent challenges. In my work in building high-trust teams and cultures, we have measured behaviors of high-trust leaders with tens of thousands of people, and almost without exception the behavior of "Listen First" consistently shows up at or near the very bottom. On average, people tend to rate themselves at 89 percent while others on their team rate them at 64 percent. The potential that rests in closing that 25-point gap would change everything.

This book provides a methodology for closing that gap that works. It isn't something that we can check off our to-do list, because it is an active, continuous process. Therefore, when we go to listen, we should do so with a genuine desire to learn. The key to influence is to first be influenced. *The Art of Active Listening* not only invites us to do this; it shows us how.

As you move forward with reading this book, I'd invite you to think about these questions: What kind of impact could active listening have on your organization? Your team? Your community? Your family? Your most important relationships?

It takes courage and consideration to learn how to listen, but the rewards for doing so far outweigh the risks. For those of us who struggle with listening, this book will be a godsend. For those who are already good at empathic listening, I would invite you to dig deeper into Heather's model. Which of her steps could make you even more effective? I'm convinced that when we hear and value others, and clearly communicate that value to them, we will see them become more invested in their relationships and organizations and leave lasting impacts throughout their work and lives.

This wonderful book codifies a process of active listening that can not only unlock team and organizational potential but also help us provide others with emotional and psychological air—creating a place where people feel genuinely heard, valued, and understood.

—*Stephen M. R. Covey*

PREFACE

• • •

Like many of you reading this book, I can recall what it felt like when someone at work took the time to listen to me and, by doing so, made me feel like I was important and what I said mattered. Similarly, I recall sitting across from a team member who needed to talk about something that was happening to them at home and how grateful they were afterward that I'd taken the time to listen to them. Then, there was the customer who vented to me for ten straight minutes about what my company could be doing better and then thanked me profusely for taking the time to hear them out.

Yet, when I look back at my career—and the various mergers, reorganizations, and internal changes I've experienced inside all kinds of organizations—I distinctly remember my coworkers saying things like "No one will listen to me. I've told them none of our customers want this new product update." Or our exasperated customers saying things like "Do you actually care what we want, or are you just assuming what we need?"

Since 2008, I've been listening to both employees and customers as an employee and customer advocate. In 2015, I launched my company, Employee Fanatix, and have been working alongside organizational leaders ever since, helping them understand what their employees need to feel fulfilled in their work. When I reflect on all the years I've spent reviewing thousands of surveys and facilitating hundreds of listening sessions, I realize I've turned into a sort of human listening database. I can honestly say, "I've heard it all." Unfortunately, that means I've witnessed countless missed opportunities when someone's failure to listen led to people feeling confused, disconnected, or even helpless. Those missed opportunities are the reason I decided to write this book.

> **I've witnessed countless missed opportunities when someone's failure to listen led to people feeling confused, disconnected, or even helpless.**

This is my third book. The first book I wrote was *The 7 Intuitive Laws of Employee Loyalty*, which was intended to be a guidebook for those who manage others to help them understand how to gain more loyalty from those they lead. The first intuitive law in that book was "Give Them Supportive Managers." In April 2021, I released my second book, *The Art of Caring Leadership*, which was mostly meant for people managers but also intended to more widely appeal to anyone who saw themselves as a leader—no matter what role they held at work. That book's main focus was to expand on the concept of being a supportive manager. In *The Art of Caring Leadership*, I wrote a chapter titled "Creating a Culture of Listening," which touched on the need for caring leaders to listen to those who look to them for guidance. Now, you have in your hands the third book, *The Art of Active Listening*, which continues to deepen this idea of being a supportive, caring leader (with or without a manager title) who actually listens to people and works to protect them from harm.

My hope is that the pages that follow will serve as a resource for anyone at work who wants to listen, and wants to listen well. That includes people who work in sales, customer service, or human resources; managers at all levels; and everyone in between. All business sectors and industries can and should learn the active listening process I outline in this book because no one is excluded from the need to actively listen at work. You'll notice that I often use we on purpose with that in mind. While I may have plenty of experience when it comes to listening,

I still see myself as someone who is a work in progress. I'm not perfect—none of us are, of course—and the point of this book is not to make anyone feel inferior. I'm

No one is excluded from the need to actively listen at work.

doing my utmost to practice what I preach.

If you read this book, I trust it will lead to great things for you. By learning how to listen well, you'll discover how to build even stronger relationships at work, which should open more doors for you, help you progress in your career, and leave you feeling more fulfilled at work. Organizations that embrace this book's teachings can expect to experience multiple positive outcomes because important stakeholders—such as employees and customers—will start to feel heard, valued, and supported, which will endear them to your organization and make them want to align with you for longer periods of time and in bigger and more fruitful ways.

At the end of each chapter, I've included invitations to reflect and consider how you'll put what you've learned into action. This will ensure that you don't stop at the theory but instead witness the powerful impact of active listening for yourself—at work and elsewhere.

The more we get this listening thing right, the more other employees will feel a sense of belonging and want to stay, and the more our customers will feel appreciated and supported by us. Ultimately, that can only lead to greater employee and customer loyalty, and a world full of people who know they matter. I don't know about you, but that's a future I can get behind.

Heather R. Younger
Colorado
September 6, 2022

HOW WELL DO YOU LISTEN?

• • •

The most basic of all human needs is to understand and be understood.
The best way to understand people is to listen to them.
—Ralph Nichols, father of the field of listening and
founder of the International Listening Organization

When I told people I wanted to write a book on active listening at work, they said things like, "Oh, thank goodness! We need that so much, right now!" Why?

Here's my theory: When we listen to someone, they receive our attention like a gift. When we hold space for them, asking questions and leading with curiosity, we send them the message that their voice holds weight and a place of importance in our heart. It's worth it, then, to get this listening thing right because it has the potential to heal so many of the divisions between us. When you think about it that way, you realize listening is our most important responsibility.

> **When we listen to someone, they receive our attention like a gift.**

During the Great Resignation of 2021, workers began leaving their jobs, in part because they hadn't felt heard for a long time. Next, they resorted to "quiet quitting"—remaining in their jobs, but with little motivation to do the work their role required because those they looked to for leadership failed to recognize their extra efforts in any definitive way and on a consistent basis. Make no mistake, customers are also quietly quitting until they find another partner who takes their real needs into consideration by listening to them.

Merriam-Webster defines the verb *listen* this way: "To hear something with thoughtful attention: give consideration."[1]

The American Psychological Association's definition of *active listening* is "a psychotherapeutic technique in which the therapist listens to a client closely, asking questions as needed, in order to fully understand the content of the message and the depth of the client's emotion."[2]

While I think these definitions highlight important elements of active listening, they also fall short. The premise of this book is that listening at work is flawed because people don't feel safe telling the truth, and listening is usually one-sided, so it rarely produces any results or the outcomes that we are looking for. You might understand the importance of making a conscious effort to hear and restate what others say, which is certainly a big part of how we need to think about listening, but the caveat is that *only* listening in this way can lead others to believe you agree with them—whether you do or you don't.

Active listening, in the way I use it in this book, is more of a doubling down, with the purpose of not only understanding another person, but also addressing any issues they raise in a way that makes them realize their opinions matter. Active listening is the doorway to increased belonging, loyalty, profitability, innovation, and so much more. It is the difference between thinking we understand what people want and knowing what they want.

> **Active listening is the doorway to increased belonging, loyalty, profitability, innovation, and so much more. It is the difference between thinking we understand what people want and knowing what they want.**

Of course, one reason we might not want to listen in the first place is because we worry that we'll hear something we'd prefer not to address. This internal resistance can often be the biggest obstacle to listening at work, and it is also why leaning in to understand

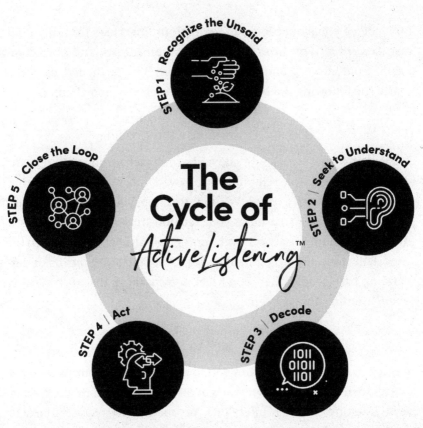

Figure 1. Cycle of Active Listening Model

isn't enough on its own. Follow-through is vital. I call this model the Cycle of Active Listening (figure 1) because the process is continuous, dynamic, and never-ending.

The Cycle of Active Listening is how we can move organizational culture forward, but it requires a strong commitment to change—not just changing how we currently think about active listening, but also how we *demonstrate* our understanding through our actions.

How This Book Is Organized

Just as the Cycle of Active Listening has five steps we need to take if we want to learn how to listen well at work, this book has five intercon-nected chapters, which lay out each step. To bring these steps to life,

I include personal anecdotes; excerpts from interviews from my podcast, *Leadership With Heart*; LinkedIn Live broadcasts; and even comments from surveys and listening sessions I've facilitated over the years. The following is a brief overview of each step and chapter.

Chapter 1: Recognize the Unsaid

Recognizing what's not being said means you pick up on the important signals. You raise your self- and social awareness to sense things that people don't expressly reveal. Without this step, you might lack understanding in an area that hurts your relationships at work. You might choose one course of action over another because you overlooked an important indicator. Recognizing what's not being said means understanding that people often don't feel safe speaking the truth. This is where listening always begins.

Chapter 2: Seek to Understand

Seeking to understand requires you to step outside of your lived experiences to uncover the perspectives of other people. You might use surveys, listening sessions, interviews, or one-on-one conversations to do this, with the intent of increasing your knowledge. By seeking to understand, you endeavor to uncover the truth, which provides you with what you need to move on to the next step in the Cycle.

Chapter 3: Decode

Decoding means taking the time to reflect on the truth you've uncovered in order to evaluate your knowledge gaps. This part of the process can be done alone or in a group. Taking time to decode indicates to stakeholders that you cared enough about their needs to be thoughtful about what you heard, instead of simply leaping into action.

Chapter 4: Act

Acting in the context of listening at work means you've taken the time to consider all data points, both qualitative and quantitative, and put together a plan of action that's inclusive of stakeholder needs. This is when momentum begins to build, and those on the receiving end of your listening start to see your commitment to their success and your desire to bring their voices to life.

Chapter 5: Close the Loop

Closing the loop means you connect the dots for those who provided you with input. You take time to let them know that not only have you heard them, but also you have a plan to take action on their behalf. You might choose to include them in steering committees or listening tours to make sure they feel included in the decision-making process and subsequent outcomes. You show people the direct correlation between the input they provided you with and what you're doing next. Not until you've arrived at the Closing the Loop stage do you know the Cycle of Active Listening is complete, and you've listened well. When you close the loop on your listening, people know without a doubt that their voice has been heard.

Unhappy Lane Hospital

I like to demonstrate our inherent desire to be listened to with the experience of a baby in a crib. A baby makes noises to signal to its caregivers that it needs something. The baby waits for them to respond, and when they do, the baby is thrilled that the sound coming out of its mouth produces an action on the part of some big people. When the people the baby relies on to meet its daily needs respond, the baby's confidence grows, its connection to its caregivers increases, and its faith in its ability to command that support strengthens. What happens, though, when a baby doesn't receive a response? It might begin to cry or scream or throw things out of its crib, all in the hopes that someone will hear it and *do* something. While people may not cry or scream at work, the emotional fallout from people not feeling heard can be equally significant.

I first started immersing myself in the study of listening at work when I was leading client development for a regional blood bank and had to survey our clients. That was followed by a stint managing customer experience for a tech company, where I helped the leadership understand what they could do better to drive customer engagement and increase sales. About six years ago, I began working for myself, helping organizations listen to their customers and employees to drive business results. The interesting thing is, during more than twenty-five years in different leadership roles, I would regularly see customers and employees wondering why those with authority failed to listen to them—no matter whether it was a failure to listen through the sales process or when a team member needed a manager's guidance. Customers and employees often provided feedback and then never heard whether that feedback made any difference. I'd hear organizational leaders wondering why those same stakeholders appeared to be disengaged or unimpressed when faced with new initiatives that bore little resemblance to what they had first recommended.

About fifteen years ago, I was working in a senior management role in customer experience. We worked with large health care systems, and there was one multimillion-dollar customer—let's call them "Unhappy Lane Hospital"—that grew increasingly frustrated with rapid changes in our delivery process. So much so that they began to reduce the number of orders they placed with us and wouldn't respond as quickly anymore to our phone calls or emails. Sometimes, they wouldn't respond to us at all.

I recognized the unsaid, and so I scheduled a time to meet with Frustrated Fiona, let's call her, a leader at Unhappy Lane Hospital, to *seek to understand* what was happening. When I sat down with her to hear her out, she gave me an earful, to say the least, but also helped me understand her concerns and prepared me to communicate those concerns to our executive leadership team. I assured Fiona that I would be in touch with next steps.

After I took her concerns back to the leadership team, we brought in other departments to discuss any changes we could make that would positively impact Unhappy Lane Hospital. After much discussion and *decoding*, we all agreed to a fair plan to *act* that included the hospital driving more of our decisions on delivery timelines moving forward.

We put different triggers in place to ensure that the issues they were experiencing wouldn't happen again. We also began rolling out quarterly reviews—not just with Unhappy Lane Hospital, but with all our larger customers, so they could provide feedback on our service delivery over a given time period. Finally, I scheduled a follow-up meeting to *close the loop* with Fiona, thanking her again for her feedback and letting her know everything we'd discussed—including the research we'd completed and where we'd landed as far as changing processes on the hospital's behalf. Fiona and her entire team were thrilled that we'd listened and decided to purchase more products from us and fewer from another partner of theirs. By listening well, our organization reaped huge benefits in the form of increased revenues and customer loyalty. Unhappy Lane Hospital transformed into Happy Lane Hospital because we took the time to listen well.

The process we followed is something any of us can do. We recognized their concerns, sought to understand where those concerns had originated from, noticed where those concerns fit into the bigger picture, took positive action in the right direction, and—ultimately—closed the loop. In other words, we followed the Cycle of Active Listening without missing a step. It all started with us committing to moving through the Cycle to serve this client in the way they expected.

Why Active Listening?
Allay Fear

A while back, I invited someone to speak on the *Leadership With Heart* podcast but found it hard to pin down a time to interview them. Time went by, and we were never able to get a conversation scheduled. A little while later, I noticed that he was on someone else's podcast, and I couldn't help but wonder how he'd found time to be on their show but not mine. I could vaguely recall him asking to speak with me in advance of scheduling a time for the interview, but my workload had interfered with my finding time for us to do so.

Fast-forward about a year, and I found myself speaking at an event where my would-be interviewee was in attendance. As I finished signing books afterward, he approached me to take a picture with him and said, "You might be wondering why I never came on your podcast but went on so-and-so's show."

"Oh, yes, I did kind of wonder that," I replied.

The next thing he said stuck in my mind as a huge failure on my part. "You wouldn't talk to me. If you recall, I asked to speak with you first, but we never managed to find the time. The other host offered to talk to me in advance of our interview to calm my nerves. I was nervous to talk to you on the podcast after listening to a couple of episodes because it seemed so easy for you. The words just rolled off your tongue. Frankly, I was intimidated."

I stood in front of him, disappointed in myself for not taking the time to listen to his concerns when I had the chance. I felt like I'd failed him, and that was a huge learning moment for me. With a jolt, I realized how my actively listening could have allayed his fears and put him at ease. I can guarantee that if *anyone* asks me to connect before an interview again, I won't hesitate to accommodate them in that way.

How many times do we fail to see how listening well might settle someone's mind and help them make more informed decisions? Luckily for me, my would-be guest decided to give me another chance. After listening to my speech at that event, watching my interactions with the audience, and tuning in to the responses I offered in answer to their questions, he felt comfortable enough to try again. We don't always get that chance. I'm just grateful I did.

Resolve Conflict

Most of us have come in contact with our own version of Frustrated Fiona—that frustrated customer (or employee or partner) who is expecting something from us that's missing. We might take time out of our day to hear that person out and even say we'll fix things, but if we don't make things right, that person will grow even more frustrated with us.

I've seen this scenario play out many times inside organizations. While it might appear that leaders are taking time out to listen to their people, they are often only *half*-listening and more attuned to their own needs than those of their customers or employees.

Here are some ways you can think about getting ahead of any slow-boiling resentment that might be bubbling up without your knowledge:

- Ask open-ended questions to indicate you're committed to understanding the other person's position.

- Lean in with compassion for what that person might be going through.

- Recognize what they *aren't* telling you.

- Take the time to research the issue.

- Come up with a plan of action to resolve things.

- Thank the other person, and relay your plan to make things better.

When we recognize that we have the power to not only make people feel heard but also use the Cycle of Active Listening to resolve conflict, we position ourselves to create win-win scenarios for everyone concerned.

Find Common Ground

Finding common ground naturally brings us closer to other people, and active listening is at its core. In contrast, when we believe no one has anything to teach us, we assume center stage in conversations and make others feel unheard. You've witnessed this if you've ever watched two people in a shouting match in which both participants want to be heard—even if that means drowning out the other person's voice by raising the volume of their own.

"I've found that a healthier and more productive way to approach our disagreements is to acknowledge that more than one thing can be true at a time," Michael Ashford, marketing executive and common-ground researcher, told me in conversation. "Cocreating new solutions to big problems fuels positive change for everyone involved."

We embrace this tension of opposites when we give up the need to be right and adopt a healthier and more productive way of interacting with the people around us by actively listening. That means taking the time to embrace curiosity and listen with an open mind and an open heart to better understand someone else's emotions, values, and lived experiences. In this way, we find common ground and avoid miscommunications.

Build Trust

"You're the best boss I've ever had."

That was the first line of an email I received after leaving one of my leadership positions. It was from a former team member who wanted to let me know how much she missed me. I have to admit I hate being called a "boss" because it makes me sound as though I'm somehow superior to those who look to me for guidance, and I never want them to feel that way. I asked her why she thought of me like that, and I will always remember her response. "You always took the time to listen to me and make sure you had my back. I trusted you, and still do. I miss you so much!"

I still get a little teary-eyed thinking about that exchange. It validates for me why listening in the right way could be the most profound thing we do for another human being.

David Horsager, author of *Trusted Leader* and *The Trust Edge*, told me that he sees listening as a foundational pillar of trust. "We know that listening shows compassion, which builds trust. Listening also creates clarity. A lack of trust is the biggest cost in any organization."

Until we commit to becoming more effective at listening to others, we'll continue to erode our relationships and miss opportunities to build something greater, together.

> **Listening in the right way could be the most profound thing we do for another human being.**

There's usually a catalyst that motivates someone to learn how to listen well. Many of us are busy putting out fires and don't always feel inclined to dig up issues not causing obvious problems. So, the catalyst might be one of the following challenges:

- A customer stops placing orders.

- An employee quits.

- A board member disengages.

- Productivity declines.

- A customer complains.

- Costly mistakes occur with alarming frequency.

Once you're aware there's an issue that can only be fixed by better listening, then you're much more willing to master the art of active listening. That said, because of the work I do in the employee engagement and retention space measuring data and sentiments and tracking for improvements, I'm a big believer that we can't master something unless we consistently practice it. That includes even when something feels uncomfortable or isn't necessarily urgent. I'll talk more about this in the next chapter.

Additional Resources

At the back of this book, you'll notice three QR codes, along with their corresponding URLs, one of which will link you to an additional resource, the **21 Days to Master the Art of Active Listening Calendar**. With this tool, you'll access daily practices that will guide you over a twenty-one-day period to practice the new skills you learn in this book, along with a way to track your progress. Keep this calendar close by, so you can access it easily in anticipation from listening to others, and stay tuned for periodic challenges by me to keep you focused on improving your active listening skills.

If you want to take what you've learned to the next level, I include a QR code you can scan to register your interest in our interactive The

Art of **Active Listening in the Workplace Workshops**, which are designed to create opportunities for team-building and collaborative learning.

Also, in that section I have created a **Video Summary** of some key strategies you can use to ensure that your learning is long-term and much more effective.

Active Listening in a Virtual World

I'm grateful to have always had a remote team, ever since starting my company. In fact, there are members of my team whom I've never even met in person. However, listening to people virtually can sometimes be more challenging than listening in person. We're forced to follow the Cycle of Active Listening through a computer screen or over the phone, where physical cues aren't as obvious—and face-to-face time isn't always an option. The good news is that the principles and steps of active listening are similar, even in hybrid or virtual work environments.

At the end of each chapter, you'll find a section that explores how each step of the Cycle applies virtually—including what to keep in mind. The Cycle's steps might seem more complicated when they have to be conducted virtually, but trust me when I say they don't have to be.

The Future of Work

In the face of new ways of working with one another, listening is more important than ever before. We can be part of the next era of work by giving others a voice, listening to them, and treating them like whole human beings.

There are so many people around us who depend on us not only to understand them, but also to do something with what we hear. In this book, I hope to expand your ability to make those in your presence feel truly heard, understood, and supported.

Ready to learn how to listen well?

Good, then let's begin.

Active listening is the doorway to increased belonging, loyalty, profitability, innovation, and so much more. It is the difference between thinking we understand what people want and knowing what they want.

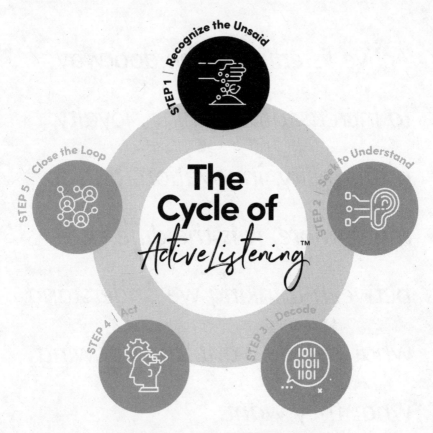

STEP 1 | Recognize the Unsaid

STEP 5 | Close the Loop

STEP 2 | Seek to Understand

STEP 4 | Act

STEP 3 | Decode

The Cycle of Active Listening™

Cycle of Active Listening Model: Step 1

1

RECOGNIZE THE UNSAID

• • •

In every story, there is a silence, some sight concealed,
some word unspoken, I believe. Until we have spoken
the unspoken, we have not come to the heart of the story.
—J.M. Coetzee, *Foe: A Novel*

Some years ago, I worked for a company that was merging five companies. The new company was spread across two countries and four states. The leadership's main focus was to maintain its monthly recurring revenue, and employee engagement was low on its list of priorities. As you can imagine, mistrust set in and communication breakdowns became rampant. Frontline managers failed to communicate status updates around the merger, so fear set in quickly. People I knew confessed to me their concerns about being laid off. Meanwhile, customers told me they felt pressured to take advantage of new product offerings. My conversations with these folks helped me realize that if the leadership team had actively listened to what people had to say regarding the merger from the start, much of the fear and stress they were experiencing could have been avoided.

When the merger was completed, people were laid off and many long-term customers left—or else shifted much of their spending. Although the layoffs may have been inevitable given new organizational priorities, the entire process could have been much more humane and less hurtful. In this case, a failure to listen hurt the organization, its employees, its customers, and many other stakeholders.

> **When you know how to listen, people will tell you *exactly* what they need to bring their full selves to work.**

After over thirty thousand engagement survey responses and years of working with organizations to transform employee engagement, here's what I've seen over and over: When you know how to listen, people will tell you *exactly* what they need to bring their full selves to work. The Cycle of Active Listening is how I help organizations move organizational culture forward, and it always starts with a first step: recognizing the unsaid.

Recognizing the unsaid means paying attention, so that you can pick up on important signals—like someone's facial expressions, body language, or tone of voice. You take time to sense what someone might be thinking but hasn't revealed out loud yet. When you make an effort to notice when someone is holding back their feelings, opinions, or ideas, you're recognizing the unsaid.

Here are some examples of things people might be thinking, but not saying out loud, where you work:

- "I wish management would show me that I'm valued here because I feel like I'm just a number to them."

- "The rapid pace of change seems disorganized, and it's stressing me out."

- "I feel like my team doesn't like me and excludes me from important conversations."

- "I'm your customer, but instead of providing what we need, you keep trying to sell us what we don't want."

- "The way you miss deadlines, or reschedule calls all the time, makes me think I'm not an important client to you."

Of course, recognizing the unsaid also comes into play outside of work. When it comes time to send our kiddos off to college, I feel like I speak for most parents when I say we always have an input or two—whether that's about the location, distance, majors offered, or something else. Like most families, we went through the process with my daughter of choosing which college she wanted to go to, attending campus tours, and doing just about everything we could to ensure that she was making the best decision for herself. My husband had suggested a school to her that he thought would be a good fit, and in the end, that was the college she chose. She said she genuinely wanted to go, and we were rooting for her all the way.

Whether she made the decision to attend this college in haste or due to the unnoticed pressure of wanting to make a decision based on the opinion of someone she admired, things didn't pan out for her in the way that any of us had hoped. After a while, she became miserable, and it started to take a toll on her mental health. As her mama, I noticed very soon that something wasn't right. I could tell she wasn't happy, but when I asked her about it, she insisted on putting on a brave face. Meanwhile, she kept trying to "sit in the muck," as I call it, but nothing about the situation ever became positive. She didn't like the atmosphere or how she had to travel the entire day to get home. Eventually, she found the courage to tell me she wanted to transfer to a school near our house. When she said she needed to make her own decision about finding a new school to attend, I felt so relieved that she'd found the courage to speak up and move somewhere she felt she could succeed, instead of staying where she was out of a sense of obligation to her dad and me.

As always, my children teach me just as much as I teach them—in my daughter's case, she reminded me of the power we have to *recognize the unsaid* when those around us are struggling or trying to send us a message. Some examples: the customer who hasn't been calling in new orders, the prospect who stops returning our calls, the coworker who has stopped contributing in meetings, the team member who has the choice to work from home or the office but only ever works from home.

The experience also made me reflect on how often people lose their voices when they start a new job. Organizational leadership steers the ship in the direction everyone must go, and people stay quiet to blend in, get along, and get ahead. This is even more likely to happen if someone has a marginalized identity and is worried about the potential negative repercussions of speaking up. If we don't do our part, these are the same folks who are most likely to leave their jobs, seemingly out of the blue—although if we'd recognized the unsaid, we'd have noticed the signs all along.

I regularly run live events where I hold space to support people as they harness the power of listening inside their organizations. During one such event, one attendee revealed there was a huge amount of frustration brewing at her company internally. Despite her leadership team setting up a roundtable for employees to talk openly about issues related to race, prejudice, and other important topics—a space they assumed would feel safe—they were met with a tumbleweed moment. The leadership team thought employees would feel empowered to speak up, but nobody seemed to want to contribute.

I reminded the attendee that progress doesn't happen overnight. Although she hadn't realized it, the tumbleweed moment was an opportunity for her to recognize the unsaid. If the leadership team had been actively listening, the message would have been clear: employees were wary about speaking up. Inviting people to a roundtable discussion wasn't enough. Instead, the leadership team needed to work to build people's trust *every* day—for example, meeting more regularly with employees one-on-one instead of in large groups, demonstrating a consistent willingness to confront hard truths, and using tough feedback to make changes. If you can show that you value all opinions, all the time—and not just the ones people *think* you want to hear—people will feel safer speaking up in the long term.

If you're interested in transforming your ability to recognize the unsaid, you must start by cultivating a listening mindset that puts you in the best position to uncover what's true.

This advice holds true no matter your position at work. If you're interested in transforming your ability to recognize the unsaid, you must start by cultivating a listening mindset that puts you in the best position to uncover what's true—and that can require patience.

Much like my daughter, we also need to recognize what we're personally leaving unsaid. If you work for a company with a culture that supports you to express yourself, and yet you don't speak up when something feels amiss, take the time to listen to what your gut is telling you before speaking to someone you trust. By taking the time to go inward, you'll become more aware of what you personally need to thrive at work. You just have to be willing to listen closely, so that you can understand your needs and act accordingly.

Cultivate a Listening Mindset

After reading many nonfiction books on communication, I've noticed that the majority focus on communicating as a way of securing what we want from others. In the context of listening, that means only listening to someone to create an outcome that works best for us—for example, a manager who only listens to an employee to determine how to drive greater productivity, a senior leader who only listens to a manager to figure out why their turnover is so high, a salesperson who only listens to a customer to figure out how to get them to buy. The problem with these examples is that they reflect a transactional listening mindset that does little to recognize the unsaid.

Recently, I was in conversation with Sarah, who explained she'd discovered that a few employees at her job had grown so unhappy they had decided to stage a walkout. The employees felt underpaid, unheard, and unappreciated. Sarah went to her manager, Kate, in confidence to let her know what was about to happen, without naming names, so Kate knew there were multiple people who felt this way. To Sarah's alarm, Kate became more concerned about who was going to walk out and how it was going to affect *her* than about actually fixing the issue at its root.

After I thought about what Sarah had shared with me, I realized there were a few things Kate could have done instead, beginning with recognizing the unsaid. Employees weren't coming to Kate directly to voice their concerns, but their proposed course of action spoke volumes. She could have faced the uncomfortable truth that people were unhappy and agreed to hear them out. Instead, she chose to focus on her ego—not on what people needed. If she had leaned into the discomfort of recognizing the unsaid, she would have cultivated more curiosity around understanding what motivated them, without being so focused on who was involved. The decision to seek out blame prevented her from finding a positive resolution.

Recognizing the unsaid often starts with facing the unknown and being prepared for whatever the truth may reveal—including when we need to take action in response to what we've learned. The temptation can be to bury our heads in the sand because we don't feel prepared to deal with what could be an inconvenient reality. Even when the truth shines a light on where we need to focus our time and energy next, it might not seem timely or convenient to do so. One lesson I've seen many organizations learn the hard way is the danger of avoiding feedback that's ill-timed. I'm rarely surprised to hear leaders express how much they regret not taking the time to address that same feedback earlier.

> **Recognizing the unsaid often starts with facing the unknown and being prepared for whatever the truth may reveal.**

In the course of one of the employee listening sessions I facilitate for clients, one participant recounted a disappointing story. During Black History Month, she decided to contact Human Resources to share her opinion on the lack of support in her company for people of color. She provided some historical context, as well as a list of professionals who could conduct workshops and training on specific topics. Unfortunately, she said, the response she received from HR was full of excuses about why the company hadn't yet made a statement of unity with Black staff members, who were feeling the strain. While the company did have an affirmative action plan, it was a plan and not a statement. When I asked her how this interaction made her feel, she said, "Invisible." She felt underappreciated, as though her opinion and voice didn't matter. "To this day, nothing has been addressed or changed."

This is at the heart of why active listening at work is so critical. This team member already harbored some anger around how her workplace did not take a stand. The HR department then missed a huge opportunity to not only recognize that this employee was speaking up on behalf of others who were struggling, but also improve the company's culture as a whole. The department's lack of acknowledgment left her feeling even angrier and more misunderstood.

Recognizing the unsaid can be an uncomfortable experience, but there is necessary growth in that discomfort. We must enter into every listening interaction with a desire to know the truth—and without assuming what that truth might be. Not only that, but once we discover the truth, we must be prepared to act on it.

> **Recognizing the unsaid can be an uncomfortable experience, but there is necessary growth in that discomfort.**

Next time you're working to recognize the unsaid, take a moment to pause and reflect on how you feel. Can you keep an objective mind and not take things personally? The more you do this, the more you'll build confidence in your ability to detect nonverbal cues from others that help you piece together what's happening beneath the surface.

Detect Nonverbal Cues

During a LinkedIn Live discussion I hosted on the importance of listening, my guest, author Chris Spurvey, described what he thinks of as the *crux* of listening: "You have got to go into an interaction with the intention of getting to know someone. We all have our intuition and our sixth sense, and so inherently start to pick up on cues, whether the other person's making eye contact or not."[1]

That intuition and sixth sense Chris mentioned can help us detect the nonverbal messages people send us to improve our listening. At the same time, we have to be careful not to make assumptions because other people's cues may differ from ours. We must pursue curiosity

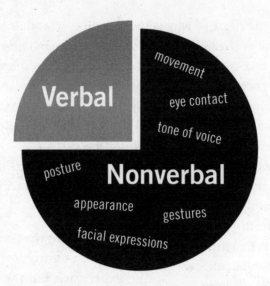

Figure 2. Nonverbal Cues to Look For

and take the time to go deeper in order to figure out if our intuition is pointing us in the right direction, or we need more insight into someone else's lived experiences. This is when we begin to *seek to understand*, which we'll talk some more about in the next chapter.

In figure 2, you can find a list of nonverbal cues to look for. Remember, these cues often tell us much more than words alone ever can. Which nonverbal cues have you noticed in the past? Which will you look for in the future?

A while back, I watched the touching movie *Coda*, which is centered on a young woman whose parents and brothers are deaf. She serves as their interpreter in everything they do. As she pursues her gift of singing, she performs in the choir at school, and her family sits in the audience, hearing nothing. They don't possess the biological ability to hear her voice, but they do look around at everyone's faces and body language and discern happiness, tears of joy, clapping, and laughter. This was a powerful scene, and while I sat there feeling sad for them that they couldn't hear her wonderful voice, I also knew they had picked up on things that most people in the room hadn't even noticed.

Later in the movie, the daughter auditions at a music school, and her parents sneak in to watch from the mezzanine. Three people are in the evaluation seats, and all of a sudden, the daughter decides to sing directly up to her parents and incorporates sign language. They are thrilled, and the evaluators, wondering what's happening, turn to look where her eyes are gazing, see her family above, and immediately understand. I loved this so much. She made those people in the evaluation seats recognize the unsaid. They had to step outside of the way they usually experienced people auditioning and allow space for something unexpected.

This story illustrates the power of using nonverbal cues to recognize the unsaid and figure out what we need to know. This is why listening in more than one way is critical—especially when people are hesitant or unable to speak up and use their voice to tell us what's actually going on. Noticing nonverbal cues means pausing long enough to see the world through someone else's eyes and noticing what's important to them.

Read between the Lines

Sometimes, we have the opportunity to recognize the unsaid in written form. A few years back, I sat across the table from Receptive Katherine, the head of HR at a financial-services firm—let's call the firm Unaware Bank—explaining to her how she needed data to understand what wasn't being said out loud by the company's employees. Her team had sent out employee surveys year after year but had never had the chance to do anything with them. When Katherine finally made time to comb through the results with my help, she had a huge aha moment. She could finally recognize what needed fixing. Unaware Bank finally understood what its people had been saying all along and began to take action to build a culture of trust in the workplace—one where people felt comfortable using their voice.

Without taking the time to read between the lines and understand what was really happening in that situation, Unaware Bank could have found itself in a precarious position: lacking understanding in an area that had the potential to harm it. The company might have chosen to change its strategic direction without having all the information, or it might have stayed the course when another type of action was required and expected. Thanks to Katherine, the right amount of time was taken to recognize what employees weren't saying openly.

Sometimes, we may recognize the unsaid and decide to do nothing about it. I recall many years ago walking up to a member of my team and dropping a new project on her desk, right before heading out to a meeting. Although I saw the stress on her face from her already long list of things to do, I still left that file with her. While I sat in my meeting, I had her frustrated facial expression stamped in my mind the entire time. I couldn't shake the uneasiness I felt and knew I had to make things right. Right after the meeting, I hurried to her office to apologize for handing off the new project in such an abrupt way without first providing context or checking to see if she had the bandwidth to take it on. Luckily, she was appreciative of my vulnerability, and we worked together to prioritize all her projects to put her at ease. In this example, I had recognized her stress and frustration, which were both unsaid. Yet, I chose to leave her with those unspoken negative emotions. While I was able to redeem myself by asking for her grace, I still regret that interaction even to this day.

Remember, recognizing the unsaid means understanding that people often don't feel safe enough to speak the truth out loud. This is where listening always begins.

If you're interested in transforming your ability to recognize the unsaid, you must start by cultivating a listening mindset that puts you in the best position to uncover what's true . . .

Recognize the Unsaid in **PRACTICE**

Creating a Safe Space in Your Workplace

Identify a time when you misunderstood a coworker, colleague, or manager at work. What did that look like? Thinking back, could you have done or said something differently? What biases did you bring to that interaction?

Use what we've discussed in chapter 1, "Recognize the Unsaid," to think about verbal or nonverbal cues you may have missed. Write below what you could have done differently.

_____

_____

_____

_____

_____

_____

_____

_____

_____

_____

_____

_____

_____

_____

Recognize the Unsaid in a **VIRTUAL WORLD**

I once spoke with a gentleman at a conference who was in sales, and he mentioned how hard it is to recognize the unsaid in the virtual world when you can't see the body language of those you interact with. "Being on the other side of a computer screen makes it a lot easier for people to hide what they are thinking."

I told him that, while that may be true, when we recognize the unsaid in a virtual world, we get to pick up on other signals and notice where someone's words and actions don't match up. For example:

- Does their expression match the conversation?
- Are they firing off an email to someone else, or fully tuned in?
- Is their video on one minute, then off the next?

Maybe you notice someone appears more distant, less focused, or not as happy as they were. Feeling isolated can do that to people. These signals can be more difficult to detect when you run your operations virtually or in a hybrid environment, but *looking* for them is vital if you want to understand and support others.

Here are a few tactical tips and strategies to help you "see" on a screen what's not said:

1. Center yourself with the mindfulness practices you'll find in the next chapter to be sure you can be fully present.

2. Set expectations around cameras being turned on or off ahead of time. You might consider making cameras-on the norm, so that everyone can do a better job of understanding one another. (Caveat: Sometimes, there are people who feel uncomfortable with cameras on for various reasons. Try to agree to specific times or situations when they are required to be on. You can also agree on times when they are less necessary, too—for example, when someone is experiencing Zoom fatigue.[2] This exercise alone will make them feel more heard and understood.)

3. Pay attention to what you see in the background in virtual meetings. Often, kids are there, pictures are on the wall, elderly parents are walking past, or animals are jumping into the picture. Take the time to mention what you see as a way to build a bridge between the other person, their home life, and your relationship with them. This will help them see you're paying attention to more than what they say and how that benefits you. (Caveat: Of course, don't use this time to poke fun at someone's home, or make them feel badly about anything that's happening in the background. Instead, always connect and uplift.)

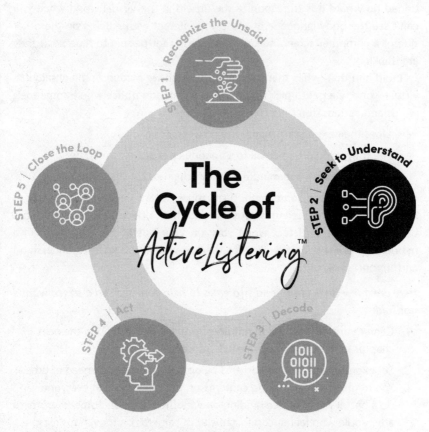

Cycle of Active Listening Model: Step 2

2

SEEK TO UNDERSTAND

• • •

If I were to summarize in one sentence the single most important principle
I've learned in the field of interpersonal relations, it would be this:
Seek first to understand, then to be understood.
—Stephen R. Covey, *The 7 Habits of Highly Effective People*

By recognizing what's not being said and then seeking to better understand the truth you uncover, you'll be in a position to move on to the
next step in the Cycle of Active Listening.

To become a better listener at work, you must seek to understand.
That means stepping outside those experiences that shaped how *you*
see the world, so you can gain an understanding of what drives other
people.

In a recent group listening session I facilitated for a client, I had an
interaction with a gentleman who was using a wheelchair. During our
exchange, he divulged how many people in his workplace would plan
parties that would be difficult for him to attend because they weren't
wheelchair accessible. While he didn't harbor any negative feelings
toward his colleagues, he did go out of his way to point it out to all of
us in the session. He also shared other examples of ways that people at
work excluded him or made him feel uncomfortable. For example, he
shared that it can be distressing to wheelchair users if you touch their
wheelchair or try to push them without their consent. The information
this gentleman shared during the session was eye-opening. While I
didn't share his lived experience, I was honored to have the opportunity

Figure 3. Key Elements Needed to Seek to Understand

to seek out greater understanding about what his life was like and how my client could improve his experience inside his organization.

Several elements must be present if you want to be successful in seeking out understanding, as shown in figure 3: curiosity, open-mindedness, empathy, presence of mind, and a courageous spirit.

Lead with Curiosity

When you're seeking to better understand others in similar ways, let down your guard enough to allow a sense of curiosity to shine through. Set your ego aside and see if you can maintain a sense of childlike wonder when listening to others. Put aside what you think might be true, and listen not for what you want to hear, but for what you want to learn.

"Curiosity shows that we appreciate the other person on the other side of the desk," Dirk Frese, VP Sales, Marketing & Service at Julabo USA, told me when I interviewed him for a LinkedIn Live broadcast. Dirk is a scientist by training, and I'm always grateful for our conversations about curiosity because he reminds me of what's true. Not only can you gain a greater understanding of a situation by cultivating curiosity, but also you can put your listening skills to good use by ensuring that the other person feels *valued*.

Something else Dirk taught me is that our brain has a chemical response to curiosity. When we exercise curiosity, our brain secretes dopamine, an important brain chemical that influences our mood and feelings of reward and motivation. In turn, when someone listens to us, we experience this same secretion. That means seeking to understand starts a dopamine cycle that benefits everyone!

The opposite of being curious is being so wrapped up in our own problems that we don't take the time to understand what's important to someone else. If you've ever been around someone who didn't give you the chance to finish your sentence before they cut you off, you know what it feels like to be on the receiving end of this treatment. This is the best way to make someone feel like you're not listening to them. By keeping the focus on yourself, you have no hope of truly understanding anyone else.

By keeping the focus on yourself, you have no hope of truly understanding anyone else.

So many people do this—often without even realizing—and I think it's for a few reasons:

- People want to be heard because it makes them feel good (that dopamine hit I mentioned!).

- People are afraid of the direction in which someone's response might take the conversation.

- People are self-centered and don't have time to learn about others in the first place.

You might be thinking, *Wow, Heather, that's very pessimistic thinking!* I would say this: I've worked in the listening space for a long time and have learned a lot about human nature and why so many of us do the things we do. Most human beings long for as many people as possible to hear them, to listen to them. This desire is innate and runs deep, but when we're seeking to understand, we *must* cultivate curiosity and put our own desires to be heard to the side—at least for the moment.

Another element critical to effectively seeking to understand others is to minimize our own assumptions about what others need, want, or intend for themselves or from ourselves.

Minimize Your Assumptions

When seeking to understand, throw out your assumptions. That means entering into a conversation as if you were a blank slate, ready to receive what might be revealed. If you're to truly give the gift of active listening, and not hijack it for your own purposes, you *have* to stop predicting what's next based on the knowledge you already have. Stay open and learn something new.

That doesn't mean you can't ever assume what people need at work based on your experiences, so that projects and initiatives can move forward smoothly. If you had to consistently stop and check your understanding, you would never get anything done. My point about minimizing your assumptions means not relying on what you infer to be true when it's time to listen in, dive deeper, and clarify your understanding.

During one podcast episode, I interviewed a leader whose story not only demonstrated the need to recognize the unsaid but also served as an example of what can happen when we lean on our assumptions without first clarifying what we think we know.[1] My guest shared that a team member of his had recently resigned. He was surprised because he thought everything was going well. She was ultraproductive and super-independent and seemed fulfilled doing as much as she was to move the business forward. When she handed in her notice, my guest was stunned. He had had no idea she was burned out. He hadn't recognized the unsaid or noticed any nonverbal cues, and so he hadn't taken the time to seek to understand. He kicks himself now because instead of sitting down with her more frequently to check in, he just assumed everything was fine. That assumption cost him an amazing employee, and that's a hard lesson for anyone to learn.

How would I propose that you know when it's time to stop relying on your assumptions? I suggest using these three questions in the decision matrix.

> If I make an assumption about what the other person's experience is, and I'm wrong, how severe might the ramifications be, and how might it impact my relationship with them?

> Would it be just as easy to reach out to the other person via email, text message, chat, an in-person interaction, or a phone call, rather than making an assumption?

> How would I feel if someone made this assumption about my wants and needs without first consulting with me?

Using this type of decision matrix will help you seek to understand, rather than lean on what you think is true, in specific scenarios. Acknowledge what you don't know—and then take accountability for your learning.

That includes noticing when you're seeking to understand only people who share the same cultural and social norms as yours. You can begin that process by asking yourself the following questions:

- Who are you predominantly listening to, or who is in your immediate circle?

- Is that group homogeneous—meaning, do you share the same cultural and social norms?

- Who has the most influence over you and the decisions you make, on a day-to-day basis?

• Do those people share your same lived experiences, or do they offer new perspectives?

• Do you tend to agree or disagree with their perspectives?

Many people see their responsibility to listen as selective in nature, meaning they can choose who is important enough to listen to and who isn't. This is the wrong way to think about active listening. Remember, *whenever* something isn't known, there's a need to seek to understand—regardless of the title or role the other person holds.

If you find yourself hesitating to ask for input from a certain individual, ask yourself why. If it's someone younger than you, for example, is your assumption that they won't be able to open your eyes to anything new? If so, consider the fact that some companies are experimenting with reverse-mentoring programs, which pair younger employees with executive team members to develop new skills and learn about issues of cultural and strategic relevance.[2] Diversify who you seek to understand across teams at work, and you'll gain insights from a spectrum of experiences you didn't have access to before.

Diversify who you seek to understand across teams at work, and you'll gain insights from a spectrum of experiences you didn't have access to before.

Similarly, if you speak to a customer who tells you how happy they are with the service your company provides, don't assume that customer speaks for all of your customers. Another customer could be waiting for the chance to complain about your slower-than-average delivery times. After receiving the first customer's feedback, you might be tempted to dismiss the new complaints, but if you do, you'll miss an opportunity to seek to understand what could be better. Challenge your assumptions at every turn, and throw them out when they don't serve your purposes of uncovering true understanding.

Recently, I was conducting an active listening workshop for a group of leaders, and I asked if anyone wanted to share a time when they didn't feel heard. One gentleman—let's call him Tim—confessed that he had felt that way before. Tim told us about a time when he'd been attending a Zoom meeting with a group of people where no one allowed him to speak or voice his concerns. Not surprisingly, he felt shut down and shut out. He noticed the lack of respect and never forgot it. When I asked that same active listening workshop group to recall a time when they felt heard, Tim piped up again to say, "I feel that way right now!"

Intrigued, I asked, "Well, what about right now makes you feel heard?"

"You're letting me speak!"

Tim's experiences get to the crux of why active listening at work is so important—and why we must take the time to be inclusive of all voices. When we give someone the chance to express themselves, they feel heard, understood, and that they belong.

Remember Receptive Katherine from the previous chapter? She and the financial services firm she worked for knew that to be effective in seeking to understand, they couldn't do it alone and needed to involve more employees. In fact, they were intentional about sending open invitations to all departments and to people in different roles to participate in multiple culture teams and customer councils. They didn't want to fall prey to homogeneous thinking, so they set out to be as open and inclusive as possible.

The opposite was true of the leadership team in the merger story from the last chapter. They were not inclusive at all in their decision-making. They didn't take the time to listen to customers or employees about ways to make the merger more successful. They kept their meetings homogeneous, with a group of people who mostly looked the same and held a similar viewpoint. No wonder the merger was such a painful process for so many.

Another key element in ensuring that we are successful in seeking to understand others is learning to grow in empathy for others' situations.

Flex Your Empathy Muscle

A while ago, my son and I went to the Department of Motor Vehicles to get his photo taken for his learner's permit. When I checked in at the counter, I realized that I had forgotten to bring his passport. I made the assumption that they only needed my ID, since he's a minor. I was in trouble with my son for making this mistake, but we spoke to one gentleman who seemed flexible. I asked if we could run home and back to keep the appointment, so my son wouldn't be disappointed. He said it shouldn't be a problem but needed to check with his manager.

My son and I watched as he walked over to his manager. That manager immediately shook his head no without asking any questions of his team member or of us. When the employee came back to deliver the bad news, I asked to speak to the manager personally. Before I could explain our situation or say one word to him, the manager immediately responded, "Sorry, ma'am, we can't do it today. It's going to be busy after school with students. You can come back another day without an appointment, but not today." I immediately felt shut down.

He could see my son's rolling eyes, but it made no difference. I left that interaction feeling like a number. I was frustrated because it felt like my voice counted for nothing. The manager couldn't care less about my situation or the fact that my son had his heart set on getting his permit that day. He took no time to seek to understand my position. True, I was the customer and the one who had made a mistake, but I would have remembered the entire exchange more fondly than I do now if he had been more empathetic and understanding—especially if he had asked me some clarifying questions, like whether I lived close enough to get home to retrieve the documents and back before our appointment time ended. He chose not to do that.

Interestingly, when we returned the next day, the employee at the counter recognized us and exclaimed, "Oh, good! You came back and got it!"

On the other hand, the manager whom we had dealt with the day before looked straight at me with apparent recognition but didn't say a word. My stomach turns just thinking about those interactions. He lacked any empathy for my son and me. I understand there are rules and policies he had to follow—it's not about that. I can take a no. But sometimes it's just about *how* that message is delivered. When someone seeks to understand where we're coming from, it completely shifts the energy running through any subsequent interaction. It makes you feel like they understand how you feel.

In this example, the manager did what I had done in my earlier example with my team member when I placed that project on her desk despite seeing her anxiety. He recognized the unsaid when he watched my reaction to the response delivered by his team member, but he ignored his responsibility to seek to understand my predicament and potentially act upon it. Instead of jumping to his own answer in his head, given a set of circumstances that he held as his truth, it would have been great if he'd set aside his assumptions and asked me clarifying questions to see if there was any workaround that could meet both his needs and mine. If he had approached the counter when he first heard my situation, slowed down the encounter to understand what I was asking, and offered understanding, I would have felt like he was more empathetic to my situation.

Did you notice that I didn't say that the manager needed to change his decision in order to make me feel heard and understood? That's because his decision to deny my request was not what I remember most about that interaction. I remember how he made me feel inconsequential and as though my voice meant nothing to him. I felt not heard but invisible. All he needed to do to change how I remember him and even how I feel about the DMV overall was to remain more flexible in his thinking and at least show an openness to have his mind changed, an openness to see me and my unique situation.

A great exercise for strengthening your empathy muscle is to intentionally notice which assumptions you make when someone speaks but you cannot actually hear what they are saying. Recently, I was facilitating a Zoom workshop with a leadership team. One of the exercises required that two people pair up in a breakout room, with one muting themselves and then telling a story about a time when they felt the most listened to. The other person was only to watch for nonverbal cues and micro-expressions. Then they switched places. Once we came back into the larger room, their responses were revealing.

Some said things like "I felt the exercise was freeing because I could say what I wanted and knew no one could hear what I was saying."

Others said things like "It felt very uncomfortable and like I was being rude because I couldn't hear them. So, I paid really close attention to what I saw and how they felt about the story they were recalling to me."

This was an enlightening exercise for everyone because it made them pay more attention to what was happening with the other person and forget about themselves for a moment. Without being able to hear, they had to sense the emotions of the other. They could really grow their empathy muscle in the process.

Empathy is sensing the feelings and pain of another. We do this to try to understand what they are experiencing. When we insert empathy into the active listening process, it helps make the conversation more about the person we're speaking with. It's more of an other-focused exercise.

An important caveat around zeroing in on empathetic listening is that, just like when you work out a new muscle, you can become depleted quickly without the proper self-care. During the COVID-19 pandemic, I grew a lot. I learned a lot about myself. I realized that I had emotional limits, and I needed to focus on filling myself up much more if I wanted to continue to support those around me. I write this because I've always been the person who leans into empathy for those around me. It's just how I was built, but being that person can take a toll, especially when you find yourself in the middle of a pandemic and racial injustice seems to be everywhere. Like many, I was trying to support my four children who were attending school remotely, my clients who were faced with working from home, and my friends who were struggling with all of this too. I could feel myself getting run-down. While it's important to practice more empathy, not less, we must understand our own limits and empathize with ourselves too.

Leaning in with empathy has more to do with quality than quantity. It's much more important to be fully present and make sure that the empathy we display is genuine.

Be Fully Present

When I was working for Mary Kay Cosmetics as a sales consultant, I never met Mary Kay Ash herself, but there were many stories about her ability to make others feel like the most important person on the planet at any given moment. I recall one scenario where someone observed her talking to one consultant at a conference while about one thousand other consultants waited in line to meet her. No matter what, she gave her undivided attention to each person standing in front of her. She gave them the gift of her presence.

What would many of us do when faced with a thousand people standing in line to speak to us? We'd most likely become frazzled, lose all focus, and appear distracted. Not Mary Kay Ash. She set out to make each person feel just as important as the next. Nothing else mattered more than being present. The people on the other end of her presence felt every bit of it too. This is something we should all aim for when seeking to understand.

I'm often told that I have presence—not in the sense of executive presence, but in the sense that I'm constantly seeking to dive deep into another person's story and life. Am I perfect at it? Nope. I remember one of my sons once saying, "Mom, it's nice that you're in the room, but you're not present." Ouch! That hurt. I struggle just like the rest of the world to truly lean in and be more like Mary Kay Ash. Nonetheless, my hope is that every person who comes to me with information, or a request, feels that I'm curious, empathetic, and present.

For example, if you're a manager, one of the most important things you can do for those you lead is set aside uninterrupted time to sit with them, one-on-one, and hear their thoughts. Help them appreciate how much you value them with your presence. There's no better way to get to know someone than to spend quality time with them. If you find

There's no better way to get to know someone than to spend quality time with them.

it hard to dedicate one-on-one time weekly, set up a monthly schedule. Take it from me: many employees don't meet that often with their direct managers or receive invites to regularly scheduled team meetings. If you want to be known as an active listener, carve out time to be present with the people who look to you for guidance and support, so that you can seek to understand them better.

At a recent speaking engagement for college advisers, one of the advisers in the audience mentioned that it would be impossible to carve out time for every student in the way I described. The advice I gave her applies to every one of us: "It's not the amount of time we spend, but the quality of the time we spend with those who look to us daily. How present are we for even just five to ten minutes when we sit with others?" When we see our presence as the main ingredient in seeking to understand, it helps us hunker down to get it right.

For those interactions that are not planned and happen spontaneously, seeking to understand requires that we more quickly clear away distractions. Can you think of a time when you reached out to someone and it took a while for them to respond? Then, when they finally responded, they were distracted? What message did that interaction send you? When you find yourself interacting with someone spontaneously, you still need to be present if you want to understand.

The problem with remaining present in any of these situations, of course, is that distractions abound—ceaseless text messages, Slack pings, phone calls, emails. There's no shortage of things that can steal our attention away from another human in need of our ear.

Recently, I was headed home from a speaking engagement and hailed an Uber. "Which airline are you flying with?" the driver asked when I got in.

"United Airlines," I replied.

"Great!"

We chatted some more in the car, and then, as we approached the airport, he asked me which airline I was flying with again. "Great, oh yes, I just want to be sure because it's a long way to walk if I drop you off at the wrong place."

Then we chatted some more and finally arrived at the airport. You know what he did? He dropped me at Southwest Airlines! I didn't notice until he'd already driven away.

Of course, it had been virtually impossible for him to be fully present with me because he was focused on driving. Talk about distracting! I share this story to underscore the importance of being present with those who need our undivided attention because it's critical if we want to ensure that we listen well and secure and retain the knowledge we seek.

So many of us think we're great multitaskers: *Let's get more done in less time by doing five things at once!* The problem with this multitasking culture is that it's ruining our ability to seek to understand at work because we're not present enough to truly listen.

Pre-COVID-19 pandemic, I must admit that I was addicted to multitasking, especially when interacting at home. My sons would come to talk to me when I was in the middle of a task, and I would look at them, then down at my screen, then over to my cell phone, and then respond. It not only drove me nuts to realize I was doing this but also sent a terrible message to my kids. The message was loud and clear: "You are not the most important thing to me right now. You will have to wait your turn to receive my attention. I can't afford the time to listen to you because I have too much going on."

I hate that I sent them that message for so long. They deserved better than that. I'm still not perfect with giving up my addiction to multitasking, but when my sons come home from school now, I shut my laptop and ask them to hang with me so that I can listen to their stories from the day, one at a time. Shut down outside distractions when you're seeking to understand someone else's perspective. When you do this, you'll send the message that the person you're listening to is who matters most.

One way to shut down distractions is to embrace mindfulness practices throughout your day. The more you do that, the more aware you become of yourself and your interactions with others. I once worked with a leader who was having a hard time focusing on his tasks, working through issues, and remaining clear about his next steps. He had never used a journal before because he didn't think it would be useful. One day, I suggested that he journal his thoughts, given what he was struggling with. Here are some of the prompts I suggested he try to help him get started on his journaling journey:

- What were my emotional triggers today, good and bad—and why? Who was present?

- What am I most grateful for?

- What did I think would get in the way of what I set out to do today?

- Where did I feel influential or in control today?

- Where did I lack follow-through?

- Where did I shine, and what was I doing?

Daily journaling is an excellent way to practice tuning out any distractions, so that you can process your own experiences—away from the never-ending ding-dings of your devices. Writing in this way can also be a great exercise in advance of a conversation you're planning to have with someone else because it allows you to bring more awareness to what you hope to learn from them.

Similarly, meditating each day can have a compound effect that increases your ability to be present. If your day has been particularly full and distracting, you might even want to pause at your desk and meditate on the spot for a few minutes. If you're anything like me, you find meditation hard to do because your mind races and you start thinking about something else entirely. I would suggest choosing a quiet time in the beginning—such as first thing in the morning before your family gets up or right before bed. There are many apps you can use to get started with meditation. Personally, I find it easier to listen to chants or spiritual kinds of music that almost hypnotize me into a sense of calm and centeredness. That is the way it works for me.

Walks in nature are also a great way to cultivate our ability to stay present. I know someone who takes as many of her calls as possible during walks outside. Being in nature allows her to explore greater depth in her conversations, as she slows down and focuses on understanding what the other person has to say and where they are coming from. I've always loved walking in nature and have often sought long walks as a refuge from stressful days that prevented me from listening to anyone—even myself.

Try blocking out time on your calendar before important meetings, even if just for fifteen minutes, so that you can clear your mind using one of these practices and show up more present and ready to understand.

Build Your Professional Courage

Many years ago, I worked with Frustrated Fiona, a leader at Unhappy Lane Hospital and a client of the company I worked for. When Fiona began to reduce the number of orders they placed with us, I knew I had to find out what was going on. I sensed she wasn't happy with rapid changes in our delivery process, and when I sat down with her to ask a few leading questions, she told me so.

Much as I wished I could run in the opposite direction, I chose to take the time to sit with her and understand her concerns. That meant summoning a lot of courage. I knew something wasn't right, and so I ran toward the discomfort of addressing it, rather than running away from it. Fiona appreciated the display of care and that I asked hard questions to understand how our services had fallen short. I continued to dig deeper, reflecting back on what I heard her say. When I left that tough interaction, she knew I'd taken her concerns seriously and understood them.

A couple of months back, I was on a plane next to someone who found out I was writing this book and felt compelled to tell me his story. As an owner of a car dealership, he recalled for me a time when a repeat customer tried multiple times to check in on the status of a car that was supposed to be on the lot. After multiple attempts to reach someone, he grew angry. He was in the office expressing that anger to a sales representative when the owner dropped into the office to see if he could mend the relationship. The owner sat with the customer and listened patiently, and then the customer said, "Thank you for listening. The car will be ready on Friday, right?" The owner confirmed that it would be. "I'll be back to buy the car when it's ready. Thank you."

That was it. All the customer wanted was for someone to sit with him, listen to his concerns, and understand him. It was that simple. Good for the owner that he gave that customer what he needed. It can be easy to overcomplicate active listening, but we don't need to. We just need to invite more courage into our interactions with people whose opinions, ideas, and insights we want to harness.

Types of Listening

As well as all the elements that must be present if we're to be successful in seeking out the truth, we also need to consider different ways of listening that can help us better seek to understand.

Active listening is about making a conscious effort to hear and understand someone else. When we actively listen, we demonstrate concern, limit our interruptions, and ask open-ended questions. We commit all of our attention to the speaker and establish an environment of trust and judgment-free engagement. At work, employees who experience being actively listened to feel a greater sense of belonging. They feel valued, appreciated, and inspired to show up for their team and organization.

When it comes to productivity, active listening has been shown to drastically improve communication and reduce the type of misunderstandings that can slow progress. In contrast, passive or distracted listening—when someone pretends to pay attention to what another person is saying but is actually thinking about or doing something else—can make people feel unimportant or unappreciated. At work, half-listening in this way can critically diminish morale. Active listening is a practice and a daily skill—not a onetime exercise—and as such it requires continual effort to generate long-term benefits.

Quick Tips to Help You Reap the Rewards of Active Listening

- In virtual meetings, avoid using your computer for anything other than the project or task at hand.

- Dedicate your full attention to conversations, and show that commitment by nodding, making eye contact, and so on.

- Be cautious of frequent interruptions, and notice who is interrupting most often.

- Read between the lines to engage with the speaker's emotions and thoughts rather than just their words (be aware of the message you're sending with your tone of voice, body language, facial expressions, etc.).

- Periodically reiterate key points in the conversation to ensure that you're fully understanding what's being discussed.

Reflective listening is a communication strategy involving two key steps: seeking to understand what another person is saying and then repeating what we think we heard back to them to confirm that we understood correctly. In a recent listening workshop, one gentleman shared that some years ago, he became frustrated by a colleague who in a meeting kept saying, "What I'm hearing you say is—" what felt like every ten seconds. "I felt less heard by her doing that. She kept parroting back to me exactly what I was saying!"

I could sense his frustration and agreed with his assessment that he was on the receiving end of someone who was practicing some over-enthusiastic reflective listening. The purpose of these types of techniques is to make listening two-way and empathetic. When we repeat back what we hear to be sure we confirm our understanding, we need to do so not in a cookie-cutter way but with the intention to let the other person know that we have processed what they said and what they didn't say and are following what they are saying. We don't need to be overly prescriptive in our approach, and we must remain aware of what others are feeling and need from us.

Phrases to Use in Reflective Listening

"You're . . ."

"It sounds like . . ."

"It seems like . . ."

"I can see that you're . . ."

"What I'm hearing you say is . . ."

Empathetic listening takes active listening to the next level because it requires us to make an emotional connection with another person and search for common ground that will enable us to respond in a meaningful way. We don't listen just with our ears but with our heart. We deliberately slow down and seek to understand with sincere intention. We don't rush to provide a solution; we simply hold space for the other person to share.

Evaluative listening is when we make a judgment about what another person says. This active listening style requires us to compare what we're hearing with what we already know or believe to be true and make careful inferences as a result.

Types of Questions to Ask When Seeking to Understand

Open-Ended Questions

Use when you want someone to tell their side of the story. In other words, you want to uncover more.

- How did that happen?
- Why did she do that?
- What happened next?
- When did that take place?
- Where did that happen?

Closed-Ended Questions

Use when you feel like you know enough, and are content with a yes or no response.

- Have you spoken to so-and-so about this?
- Do you know what to do next?
- Are you OK figuring things out from here?

Whatever blend of listening styles you adopt in your bid to seek to understand, remember it's all about practice. You can practice by constantly leaning in, paying attention to both nonverbal and verbal cues from others, and putting your skills to the test by following up to see if you understood correctly.

How to Seek to Understand

When a company I worked for began rolling out quarterly *partnership reviews* for its customers, we discovered how well the reviews secured valuable information we needed to improve while making the customer feel valued. Today in my speaking and consulting business, I still use a partnership review when meeting with long-term clients, so that I can go over their concerns, highlight any wins, and uncover strategic opportunities to strengthen our business relationship, among other things. I use the word *partnership* because I always think of myself and my organization as a partner to our clients. We're on a journey together, and both of us share the same goals to see them succeed.

The main focus of these reviews is to do a lot of active listening and ask the right questions of the client while I'm in front of them. Some questions I might ask include the following:

- How do you feel this partnership is going?

- How can we improve as your partner?

- Have there been any service issues we're not aware of?

- What do you want to bring to our attention that we may not have noticed?

After I ask these questions, my goal is to listen to their responses and notice what is not expressly stated.

Many of my clients set up *customer councils*, which are a type of market research undertaken with a cross-section of customers on a regular basis. Customer councils can be extremely helpful when gathering thoughts on new products or services, user trends, or company priorities—and a properly designed and well-orchestrated council meeting can provide value many times greater than the investment of putting one together. Satisfaction surveys and suggestion boxes work in much the same way, with an added layer of anonymity that helps garner more honest feedback.

Internally, an excellent way you might seek to understand is to hold team meetings or roundtable discussions to discuss key issues, during which you ensure that everyone's voice is heard and given equal importance. People who are used to receiving the message that their voice matters most can often hijack these types of discussions because they are so eager to express their opinions. Facilitating these types of meetings with awareness of these dynamics is critical for those of us who want to be better listeners, as we have a responsibility to keep discussions balanced and fair.

Stay interviews are informal conversations that can unlock valuable information about what an employee enjoys about work. If leaders navigate these types of conversations in a way that makes an employee feel safe, that person may also venture their thoughts around what could be better. Far better for them to feel able to share this information with you early on than wait until it's too late, and you instead find yourself conducting an exit interview.

At the same time, *exit interviews* have their own value, if performed by a leader who values seeking to understand and can be patient in learning from the other person what went wrong and how the leader might avoid replicating such scenarios in the future. These types of interviews require the leader to listen without becoming defensive. When we're defensive because we don't like what we hear or perhaps don't agree with what we hear when we hear it, we send the other person the message that their voice holds no value to us. This is the antithesis of active listening.

When Things Get Heated

Seeking to understand is easy when things are calm and no one is angry, but how do you actively listen when someone is angry or upset?

When you recognize that emotions are heightened, here are some best practices to consider.

Put It in the Parking Lot

Sometimes, when we're in group meetings, in one-on-ones, or even on calls with clients, we reach an impasse when two parties can't see eye to eye. This is the best time to agree to place something in the parking lot. I never used to understand this concept before, until I reached a deadlock with a colleague. We couldn't seem to accept the other person's perspective, but we knew we needed to put the issue to one side for the moment, reflect on what we'd both shared, and take time to understand the other person's side of things.

The parking lot was the best place to table the discussion, so that we could return to it later without completely downplaying its importance or making the other person feel like their viewpoint or concerns were invalid. Putting something in the parking lot for a later discussion doesn't minimize the issue or eradicate the discussion; it merely delays it. That way, all parties can reconvene later with a clearer mind and their emotions in check.

Walk Away with Respect

There are other times when the best decision you can make for yourself is being the one to respectfully walk away (see figure 4)—or respect

Put It in the Parking Lot

Walk Away with Respect

Agree to Disagree

Figure 4. Best Practices When Things Get Heated

someone else's decision to do the same. Ask yourself, "Do I see us coming to a conclusion here?" If your answer is no, it might be time to let things go. Sometimes, the longer the discussion is allowed to continue with no resolution in sight, the worse things become.

Walking away with respect doesn't necessarily mean you're running from or avoiding an issue. Instead, there are times when you need to listen to the voice of reason in your head that's telling you the discussion has moved into destructive waters and it's best if everyone jumps ship. No good can come from minds that are blinded by anger or feeling misunderstood. Walking away is sometimes necessary to keep your sanity—especially when a group of people is involved and the conversation isn't progressing in a useful way for anyone. Hopefully, everyone can understand the gravity of the situation and respectfully follow suit.

Agree to Disagree

Agreeing to disagree is one of the hardest paths to choose in a heated discussion. We all want to be heard and understood but, most of the time, just want to be right. Although agreeing to disagree may sound simple, it takes effort to accept that neither party will come to a clear finalization of the topic at hand.

I remember a group of friends chatting about Major League Baseball, and each of them was from a different part of the country, so naturally many were fans of baseball teams from their home states. Two of them happened to be fans of rival teams, and just when I thought the discussion was going in the direction of playful banter, it turned into a heated debate. Their friendship was tarnished by this sudden disagreement. This is a great example of how agreeing to disagree could have not only prevented this argument but likely saved their relationship.

The truth is, you can't agree on everything. Focus on what matters, and let the small things go. Ask yourself how important an issue really is. Are you compromising your beliefs or morals? If yes, it's important that you effectively and respectfully explain why you think your values are impacted and how this makes you feel. If not, maybe it's time for a trade-off. Consider why the other person has a different view of the situation and outcome.

- Why are they upset?

- What does the issue look like from their point of view?

- Is there a way your behavior can change to positively impact them?

You'll always be faced with arguments or disagreements. They are an inevitable fact of life. There will be times when you'll be able to work things out, and there will be times when you'll need to take the high road. The world wouldn't be what it is without other people's opinions, ideas, or voices. We all want our voices to be heard—isn't that why arguments start in the first place? It will help to ask these three questions the next time you feel lost in battle.

Who's Responsible?

Everything I talk about in this book applies to anyone at work who interacts with anyone else. *It's that simple.* Even if you don't personally hold a formal leadership position, you still have a responsibility to seek to understand the people you work alongside.

I always say we have more power and influence than we think to make others feel a certain way. People stay at their jobs because of the relationships they build at work. Conversely, if they don't feel connected to others, they are less likely to stay. Think about the daily interactions you have with your coworkers, whether during a Zoom meeting, email exchange, or group meeting. Are you doing everything in your power to ensure that other people feel understood and listened to?

Once you gather invaluable insights by seeking to understand, you'll be able to reflect on your next steps before deciding which action to take, if any. That starts with the next step in the Cycle of Active Listening and the next chapter, "Decode."

Seeking to Understand in **PRACTICE**
Exercising Mindfulness at Work

Identify a time when you feel that you didn't seek to understand, and a time when you did.

How were they different? Jot down what differences you can recall.

By doing this, you can identify what mindfulness practices you need to insert into your day to clear enough headspace to better understand the people around you at work. Some people need to work out daily, some need to eat a big breakfast, some need to meditate in the morning before going to work.

Reflect below on what you need in order to seek to understand others.

_____

_____

_____

_____

_____

_____

_____

_____

Seek to Understand in a **VIRTUAL WORLD**

On a productivity level, seeking to understand drastically improves communication and reduces instances of misunderstanding that can slow progress. This is especially critical if you're working in a hybrid or remote environment.

Here are a few tips and strategies for you to call upon in a virtual or hybrid work environment:

1. If you notice someone has seemed off lately, or their productivity seems below average, reach out and check in. Most of the time, they might just be looking for a reprieve from the stressors of the day, especially if they have a lot on their plate. They may also feel too busy to ask for help. Or, things might not be going well at home. Your genuine asking shows that you're seeking to understand. If people then feel safe enough to be up-front and honest with you, you contribute to building a foundation of trust, safety, and transparency at work, which benefits everyone.

2. Next time you're on a video call, physically lean into the screen. You don't have to look directly into the camera, as that can feel too forced. Instead, stare intently at them on the screen while you lean in, so they can see that your eyes are fixed for active listening. (Caveat: If you're interacting with someone who has the camera off, you should still take the posture above, as they can see you. Don't use the fact that their camera is off as an opportunity to become distracted. Ask them more questions to clarify your understanding.)

Seeking to understand in this way sets the tone for a virtual culture of listening and a close-knit team. You can help eliminate the sense of isolation that people working virtually can experience and create a greater sense of connectedness and belonging.

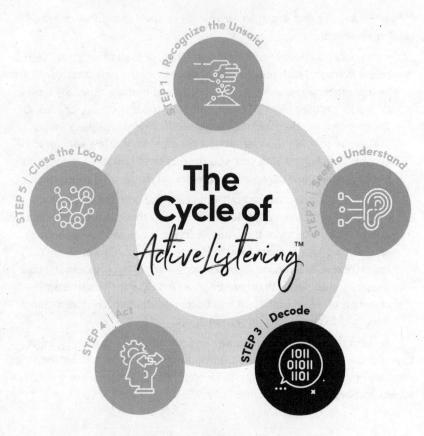

STEP 1 | Recognize the Unsaid

STEP 2 | Seek to Understand

STEP 3 | Decode

STEP 4 | Act

STEP 5 | Close the Loop

The Cycle of Active Listening™

Cycle of Active Listening Model: Step 3

3

DECODE

• • •

*Reflection doesn't take anything away from decisiveness, from being
a person of action. In fact, it generates the inner toughness that you
need to be an effective person of action—to be a leader.*
—Peter Koestenbaum, interview, *Fast Company*, February 29, 2000

One of the most powerful things I've witnessed time and again through
my career is seeing the energy rise in employees and customers when
they realize that what they have to say matters, and other people are
genuinely interested in their perspective.

"A leader's job is to take the time to listen to everyone and harvest
the team's best ideas from there," Chuck Runyon, cofounder and CEO
at Self Esteem Brands, shared with me on my podcast. Whether you
consider yourself a leader or not, you need to manage expectations and
communicate when you can't solve every problem at once. Discerning
which action items you will act on first, if any, is something you need
to think carefully about if you want to avoid overpromising or getting
people's hopes up. I call this process of discernment *decoding*.

Tell me if this sounds familiar. You receive feedback from your
spouse, kids, coworkers, boss, or whomever, and immediately jump into
action without first considering what the best plan of action should be.
I know I've been guilty of this. To ensure that you're actively listening, you must slow down and take the time to decipher what someone
tells you. That means interpreting what you've heard. Decoding is your
opportunity to connect the dots between what someone said and what
you should do about it. When you decode, you have the opportunity

Decoding is your opportunity to connect the dots between what someone said and what you should do about it.

to identify those changes that are likely to have the greatest impact. In other words, decoding allows you to see the complete picture.

I once had a team member who thought I should offer more expanded days of paid time off to remain competitive with other organizations. When she first approached me with this idea, I immediately felt inclined to say no. The current paid time off package I offered had been assembled by an HR professional, and I felt it was fair. Instead of saying no, though, I thanked her and said, "Let me take a few days to do some research and get back to you."

I'm glad I did! It turned out my competitors were offering way more paid time off than I was. The team member's request was fair. I was more than happy to give her and the rest of the team additional days off. We both walked away happy because I had taken the time to decode, assemble a plan of action, and report back. She was happy to receive an additional five days off each year, and I was happy to provide them.

What might have been the alternative? I could have shut down the team member's request because I felt she was taking advantage of my generosity. That would have left her feeling unheard. Instead, I did my due diligence and found she was right to ask for those additional days off.

As you think about how to master the art of active listening, remember the importance of decoding before you take action, so that you know what to do next. You might be tempted to jump to conclusions, but instead give yourself space to interpret what someone shares with you. Reflect on what you hear before choosing whether and how to act. This reflection period lets the people in your presence see how important they are to you and helps you make informed decisions that will benefit more people in the long run.

How much reflection time is enough? There is no formula or cookie-cutter approach to deciding how much time you should take. We only have so many hours in a day, and I understand if this new way of listening feels time-consuming. Just know that the process is worth it, and the time commitment always depends on the circumstances. It's more important that you be intentional about following the decoding process rather than following some preconceived time frame.

Benefits of Decoding

The benefits of decoding are numerous. I want to take time to lay out two of them, so you can understand what a critical role decoding plays.

Uncover Flawed Thinking

How many times have you left a meeting after a heated debate and realized you were on the wrong end of an argument? This type of realization happens to the best of us. That's why people warn against making decisions when we're angry, because emotion often clouds our ability to come to the right conclusions. While it can be difficult to admit when you're wrong, people respect you when you find the courage to acknowledge any flawed thinking and move on with a plan to address any oversights.

A colleague of mine once recalled a time when he discovered the company he worked for was losing millions of dollars due to incorrect data processing. All the explanations those responsible gave about why this was happening were highly technical. Yet when my colleague took the time to research the issue more closely, he found an anomaly and brought it up to the leadership team. The team talked it over and asked my colleague to dig deeper to fix the problem. They heard him, decoded what he reported, and acted upon it. He felt truly empowered as a result.

Those responsible were sure they were right, but the decoding process revealed that the way they were thinking about it was wrong. Losing millions of dollars could have been avoided had the leaders decided to decipher the technical research when they first had the opportunity.

How should you handle things if, after decoding, you find out your assumptions were wrong? The first step is to release your initial desire to prove you were right, own your mistake, and reenter the conversation with more humility. The second step is to admit your error to anyone who felt wronged by your assumptions, so that they see you're taking responsibility for your inaccurate thinking and behaviors. Approaching this type of situation from a place of vulnerability will help you build trust. This is the gift that decoding offers you, after you've completed your research and taken time to reflect.

Some years back, I had a dispute with a colleague who swore I had withheld information on purpose that would allow her to make a different decision at work. To this day, I don't know how she made that assumption, but it happened. I tried to convince her that I had had no ill intent when forgetting to tell her that piece of information. In fact, the information hadn't seemed important to me, and I mistakenly assumed that it wouldn't be important to her either. For a couple of months, she didn't want to talk to me, which left me plenty of time to reflect on my assumptions. My guess is that she also needed that time to reflect on our relationship and our history of friendship, and decide whether she thought my heart was in the right place. Time went by, and she seemed more and more receptive to hearing my side of the story. When we finally reconvened to talk about things, we were more ready to approach our disagreement with objectivity and better reasoning. She was able to see my heart and realized that I had had no intention to hurt her or leave her out. I admitted that I needed to be much more sensitive to differing priorities. Since we both took the time to process our initial conversation, we were able to see each other's side and maintain our close relationship.

Decoding is a classic example of slow thinking. Slow thinking engages our frontal cortex and isn't hijacked by our amygdala, which rules fast thinking. I call decoding an example of slowing down to speed up, which for someone like me—a hyper-achiever and fast mover by nature—can be incredibly hard to do. What sells me on slowing down enough to decode is knowing I'll be more likely to avoid costly mistakes or communication breakdowns like those cited in the examples.

In a stressful workplace culture where other people expect you to always be on, it can be extraordinarily hard to slow down enough to decode, but the risks of short-cutting the decoding process are never worth it. This is why doing your part to create a culture of active listening, where

The risks of shortcutting the decoding process are never worth it.

data-driven thinking takes precedence over quick wins, is critical if you want to avoid burning yourself, and other people, out. When you encourage others to take the time they need to make the most informed choices available to them, you empower them to contribute and take responsibility for their contributions.

Increase Collaboration

I've been told a few times in my career, meant partly as a compliment and partly as a slight, "Heather gets more done by 9 a.m. than most people do in a day!" The compliment is that I'm extremely productive and have tons of energy, but the slight is that I get a lot of stuff done by myself.

I have to admit that while I love connection and other humans, I don't always lean into collaborating with others for the sake of getting things done. Having said that, I've learned in the last five years of building my own business that we can get only so far alone. I've embraced collaboration, and it's empowered me to do more than I ever could have by myself. For example, a couple of years ago, I realized I could no longer keep track of posting on social media and writing weekly blog posts. So, I hired expert team members and leaned on other resources to help me accomplish those tasks. Learning to relinquish control over different things on my plate helped me learn to trust the gifts of others and enjoy more time for family and self-care. The best part is, those experts often catch things I don't. Collaborating with them in this way helps me stay on my leading edge, and for that I'm grateful.

When you include more people in the process of decoding the information you receive, you have the chance to uncover connected problems and gain additional insights. Certain problems may never surface if you choose to act alone instead of collaborating.

I remember one time when I worked in customer experience, a client provided us with feedback about how the application she was using failed to perform a certain task, despite our promising the application would work without a hitch. I went in to test the issue on my own and thought I had discovered the problem. I circled back to the customer and explained to her that I knew what the issue was, and we could fix it. What I didn't know—because I hadn't told anyone initially about the issue, nor did I include anyone else in my decoding process—was that five more customers had already complained about the same issue. The development team had already discovered something much larger than what I had found.

If I had decided to include more people in the decoding process, I would have known that. Instead, I had to go back to the customer and let her know the problem was much more complicated and would take longer to resolve. Instead of making her feel confident in my abilities, I lost credibility with her and had to work twice as hard to earn it back.

Practical Tips for Decoding

It can be hard to find the patience to decode effectively. I make excuses all the time for why I don't need to take the time to fully consider what I've heard. I've also seen the positive impacts of making decoding a priority. How can you ensure that you take that time?

1. First, remember that when someone shares something with you, they give you the gift of knowing what their wants and needs are. When you handle their words with care, you give *them* a gift in turn. When you keep this in mind, it will help you mentally prepare to decode from a place of understanding and gratitude.

2. Next, never underestimate the power of blocking out time on your calendar to reflect on what you've heard. That might mean you send out an invitation to others suggesting you discuss the issue, or you go out of your way to research what you need to know on your own. I'm not suggesting you take hours and hours

to do this, although occasionally that is required. This could take as little time as thirty minutes to handle the information that has been entrusted to you.

3. Lastly, come up with a set of questions you want to reflect on each time. So, for example, those could look something like the following:

What does this person require of me?

Do I need to involve others?

Do I need to do something about this feedback?

Have I heard this feedback before? If so, how was it addressed?

Where can I find out more information about this?

These are just some examples. The point is, you take the complexity out of the decoding process if you set in place a framework for reflecting.

Make your decoding time count by keeping an open mind when you're doing it. Remember that your thoughts are just that: your thoughts. If you set aside time to decode on your own or set meetings to discuss it with others, but already have a preconceived idea of what the outcome should be, then decoding will be a waste of time. On the other hand, if you make time to decode what you hear, and you understand that you might have to alter the way you think about things based on new information you uncover, you put yourself into the best possible mindset to interpret what you've learned.

What If I Don't Decode?

During the major company merger I went through, the private equity firm wanted to change an established and in-demand product. The problem was, they underestimated the loyal client base that the original product had acquired over a span of twenty-five years. The firm pushed hard to make changes to the original product but never asked customers if they wanted the change or asked employees what they knew.

In the midst of all the changes that took place, many long-term employees did begin to share feedback about what they heard from customers, but no one wanted to listen to what they had to share. On the rare occasion that someone *did* listen, that person rarely took the time to reflect on the incoming waves of feedback.

What messages did these leaders send?

- "We know better than you do."

- "You just sit there while we do our thing!"

- "We don't really respect how you feel about these changes."

- "Your opinion has no bearing on our next steps."

When you fail to interpret what you hear from people at work as a leader, you send them the message that they are inconsequential cogs in a big machine and not important to you or your organization. If you want to bring those people along and make them feel invested in the direction you're taking, they have to feel that they have a voice in the destination.

When you fail to interpret what you hear from people at work as a leader, you send them the message that they are inconsequential cogs in a big machine and not important to you or your organization.

In the case of the organization I was working for, they didn't discover the value of listening until it was too late. They thought they knew better than those who were on the front line serving clients. They even thought they knew better than the customers. The merger failed in short order. This was the price they paid for making knee-jerk decisions to move forward on plans without consulting others and failing to fully evaluate other people's concerns. Those in charge assumed they knew what was best, and that ultimately resulted in a failed merger.

In contrast, when I worked with Frustrated Fiona at Unhappy Lane Hospital, I took the feedback she gave me and handled it like it was the most valuable diamond I had ever seen. By doing so, I signaled to Fiona the utmost respect for our relationship. I processed her feedback alone for a short time and then began to meet with other individuals at my company in different departments to validate her complaints and seek solutions with those who were closer to the problem. I had only done my job once I had discovered all that I needed to return to Fiona with a viable way forward. I explained to her all the steps I had taken to make sure I understood her concerns. I had been thorough, and she could see that I took her grievances seriously. She became more loyal to me as a result, and our two organizations began to work together more closely because I had gone through the decoding process. I didn't hide the effort I went to on her behalf, and I made sure to include her in both the process and the solution.

Unconscious Bias

I've mentioned the role of assumptions several times in this book because incorrect ones can immediately halt the active listening process and prevent us from learning anything new. Beyond this, making assumptions at work can be divisive, cause conflict, and foster hard feelings and even complacency. When we make assumptions without additional context, we're more likely to feel or react defensively—even if our reaction is inaction.

We refer to unconscious biases as those assumptions we make about other people without realizing, even when we don't intend to. We tend to develop these biases based on our personal experiences, as well as messages we receive over the course of our lives from the media and people around us. Often, these biases affect how we perceive, interact with, and listen to others, but they can be brought to the surface and examined in the cold light of day. When we do that, we often see that our biases were unfounded or that we were missing an important insight or perspective that could have helped us see things differently.

Unconscious bias plays a role in decoding, as it requires us to be honest about the way we look at the world and take the time to fully understand where someone else is coming from when their experience doesn't reflect our own.

> **Unconscious bias plays a role in decoding, as it requires us to be honest about the way we look at the world.**

Sometimes, what we discover about our assumptions and biases can be unsettling. That emotional reaction can lead to a shame spiral that can be hard to recover from. For example, you might realize you draw conclusions about people based on their age, gender, race, ethnicity, or weight, or the type of car they drive. Now that you know better, you can be more mindful about the stereotyped views you hang on to.

If you've ever been on the other end of a conversation with someone who made up their mind about you without knowing you, you know what it feels like to not be fully seen for who you are. This is what it feels like for people when we fall into the trap of making biased assumptions, and it is a great reminder that we can't do this work *unless* we get to the bottom of what we don't know.

Decoding, by its very definition, is more successful and productive when done with others who share different perspectives. When you do that, you have the chance to achieve a greater level of understanding *before* you jump to any conclusions.

One of the greatest questions you can ask to overcome any hidden biases is "What am I missing?" By asking yourself this question and involving others in your process of inquiry, you expand your perspective and invite greater understanding. When you believe there's more to learn, you create opportunities to consistently gain knowledge. When you decode with this mindset, you prepare yourself to take action on what you've heard in a much more effective way.

When you fail to interpret what you hear from people at work as a leader, you send them the message that they are inconsequential cogs in a big machine and not important to you or your organization.

Decoding **REFLECTIVE PRACTICE**
Evaluating Your Reasons for Decoding

Identify a specific time when someone at work made a knee-jerk reaction that negatively impacted you, your work team, or a customer. Now, recall when you were tempted to jump into action but took time to reflect on input you received instead.

Write down what was happening in the environment.
- Who was involved?

- What made you pause?

- Is there some way that you can re-create this environment on your own?

- How could this become a consistent practice at work?

With as much detail as possible, lay out a plan for how you can be consistently successful in decoding going forward.

_____

_____

_____

_____

_____

_____

Decode in a **VIRTUAL WORLD**

Decoding virtually carries the same risks as decoding in person. If you rush ahead, jump to conclusions, or rush into action, you won't give yourself enough time to recognize and interpret what's actually going on. Remember to pause and build into your calendar time for careful reflection.

Here are some practical tips for decoding in a virtual or hybrid work environment:

1. Slow down to speed up. That means fully considering the pros, cons, and implications with others if you can, so that you make more informed decisions that benefit everyone in the long run. This might entail multiple Zoom meetings with different people to truly get to the bottom of things, so that you can benefit from others' insights and ideas before coming up with your final response.

2. Step away from the screen, the chat box, your cell phone, and anything else that keeps you distracted to truly ponder what has been said to you by others. It's that quiet space that will allow you to wholeheartedly take in everything and see angles you might not otherwise when glued to a screen.

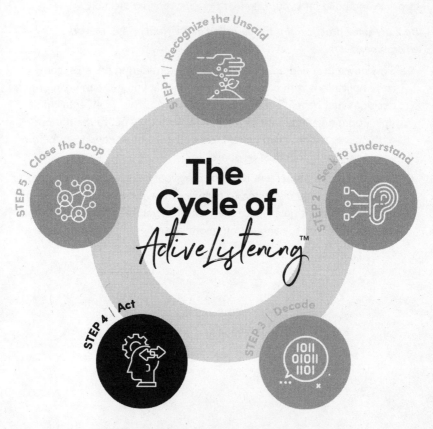

The Cycle of *ActiveListening*™

STEP 1 | Recognize the Unsaid

STEP 2 | Seek to Understand

STEP 3 | Decode

STEP 4 | Act

STEP 5 | Close the Loop

Cycle of Active Listening Model: Step 4

4

ACT

• • •

Take time to deliberate, but when
the time for action has arrived,
stop thinking and go in.
—Napoleon Bonaparte

There is a time to decode, and then there is a time to act—in that order. Taking action after you've followed the first three steps in this book is the difference maker when it comes to listening. That means signaling to others your commitment to help them. One act alone can send someone the message that they are valued, important, and more than just a means to an end.

Think back on a time at work when you told someone you needed them to act on something, but they never did. How did that make you feel? Unheard? Unimportant?

Now, think back to a time when you told someone you needed them to act on something, and they did take action on your behalf. How did *that* make you feel? Heard? Important? Maybe less alone?

We need to remember that for every action we take, there is an equal and opposite reaction. I'm sure that at some point in your life, you've heard of Newton's famous third law of motion—or, as it's more commonly known, the law of action and reaction. Just as jumping applies a force to the ground and the ground propels you into the air, so you can view the actions you take in response to active listening at work. When someone at work voices their concerns, and you act by hearing them out, you're likely to receive a positive reaction—such as a strengthened relationship and maybe even increased productivity or engagement. On the other hand, if you choose not to address that person's concerns, the consequences of your inaction will likely entail a negative reaction—such as a weakened relationship, low morale, a lost customer contract, or even someone's resignation.

One day, a team leader of mine—let's call her Jaded Jen—came to me frustrated and disappointed over what she saw as the highest form of deception. At the time, Jen and her team were in customer service and answered all the calls that came into the business. As the team leader, Jen could access call logs, so she could audit conversations and coach the team on areas they could improve in. One day, Jen was listening in on calls and heard two coworkers, both who reported to her, talking in a disparaging way about her on the recorded line. Jen brought this to my attention, and I agreed to listen to the recordings. When I did, I couldn't believe what I heard. I dropped by Jen's office to let her know that I understood the issue and would need to take some time to decide how I would act.

I took a few days to think about what my next steps were going to be, speaking with HR, conferring with my manager, and researching similar scenarios on online forums. Next, I called the two coworkers into my office one by one to discuss what I'd heard. They were each baffled to be called in, as they had forgotten that their conversation was being recorded. What could they say? There was no way to justify their blatant disrespect. I told them both that their actions were counter to our agreed-upon values and, for the first time in my leadership career, wrote them up for their behavior. I needed them to know that I wouldn't settle for such behavior on the team. I let them both know that I'd do the same if someone disrespected them in the same way. While they seemed frustrated, they also appeared disappointed in themselves for letting me down. Afterward, I followed up with Jen and let her know that I had taken action to resolve the issue. Jen appreciated my taking her concerns seriously. I was appreciative of the opportunity to show Jen that I valued her loyalty to the entire team and defend her in this way.

Even though we haven't worked together for many years now, Jen and I are still close to this day. While this whole situation wasn't an easy one to act on, I would do the same if I had to again. I needed Jen to know that I heard and valued her, and that was why I did what I did.

It's Not the Size of the Action That Counts

When I speak to people about the need to act as a part of the active listening process, I'm often asked how much responsive action I recommend. I always explain, as in figure 5, that it's not the *size* of the action that counts but the *intent* behind our actions—and the alignment of those actions to the person's original request. This is what determines an action's impact. That means your impact could be the same whether the action you take is big or small. The question to ask is, "Do my actions align with the person's expectations and meet their needs?"

Our decision to change our delivery processes without consulting Fiona at Unhappy Lane Hospital caused a backlog in the business she sent our way and eroded her trust. If, after hearing all of her feedback, I had gone back to her with yet *another* change that didn't meet her needs, I would have made the situation much worse. Even if I had good intentions, the impact of my actions wouldn't have aligned with her expectations. I had to listen to her first and seek to understand what she expected, *before* I could act.

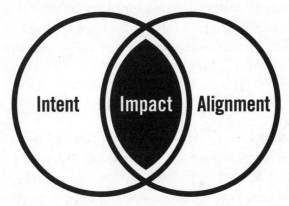

Figure 5. When to Take Action Decision Matrix

Three Steps to Sustainable Change

No matter how committed you are to taking action, you have to be sure you can sustain it. There have been many times when I've worked for organizations that wanted me to believe they were action-oriented and open to change. Whenever there was a new change initiative, there would be a collective rally to let people know what was coming, which would lead to a constant buzz around the office. People would excitedly debate the anticipated result of the initiative. Eventually, the big day would come, and the organization would roll out its changes. Mandatory meetings and trainings would fill the next few weeks in an attempt to get everyone up to speed and on board with what was happening. During this time, people would sometimes have the opportunity to share their thoughts about what was happening, but that didn't always occur, especially if everyone was swept up in rolling things out. Another couple of weeks would go by, and before you knew it, the buzz would subside. Normal work habits would resume, and after a time, no one would speak about the big change initiative anymore.

> **No matter how committed you are to taking action, you have to be sure you can sustain it.**

Difficulty sustaining changes happens when there isn't a system for implementation or a way to track progress. In fact, approximately 50 percent of all organizational change initiatives are unsuccessful, which is why knowing how to plan for, coordinate, and carry out change is a valuable skill for anyone at work.[1] Here are three proactive steps you can take to ensure that the changes you implement are sustainable.

1. Recognize the Need for Change

When you follow the Cycle of Active Listening and take time to recognize, understand, and decode the need for change, this step is usually the easiest. Whichever problem you're experiencing, even if you're aware of the issue but unsure of its origin, I assure you that *someone* knows the root cause. Other people can be your greatest asset when it

comes to diagnosing a problem and its source. That's why it's impera-
tive to ask the right questions and listen to what people tell you.

In order for my client Receptive Katherine, the head of HR at
Unaware Bank, to recognize that change was necessary, she first had
to become aware of what the problem was by combing through the
results of thousands of employee surveys. Once her company accepted
that there were things people were not saying out loud that could make
the workplace culture better, they leaned into the Cycle of Active Listening to meet that need for change head-on.

I think this concept is easier to understand when we consider personal life goals, like remaining healthy. I don't know about you, but I
often recall my commitment to my health when I look at my children.
I know I want to see them grow up and have families, and I also know
that my good health directly correlates to my ability to meet that life
goal. I knew there were holes in my plan when I saw some objective
health information that helped me understand where I was going off
course. Now, I do certain things consistently to stay in good health.
I recognize the need to change habits that don't serve me, because I
know my "why" for pursuing change. Whether you're a senior leader, a
front-line team member, or a midlevel manager, you'll become clearer
about the need for change if you can recognize the need for doing so.

2. Cultivate a Desire for Change

We're hardwired to resist change. In fact, our bodies want to protect
us from it—hence they release stress-induced hormones that make us
fight, flee, or freeze. When you
experience resistance to change,
take a moment to observe
what you're experiencing. Our
thoughts govern how we feel,
so pay careful attention to how
your perceptions of a situation might be shaping your emotions.

> **We're hardwired to resist change. In fact, our bodies want to protect us from it.**

- In fight mode, you might catch yourself thinking, *This is never going to go the way I want!*

- In flight mode, you might find yourself thinking, *I don't have time to worry about this right now!*

- In freeze mode, you might think things like, *What if I'm wrong, and this isn't the change that's needed at all?*

Your awareness of how you're feeling, and your willingness to work through that, is an essential part of taking action. In fact, you won't move forward until you've addressed any internal resistance that surfaces.

Greg Faxon, author of *Don't Let the Fear Win: How to Get Out of Your Own Way and Grow Your Business . . . Fast*, recommends asking the part of yourself that's in fight-flight-or-freeze mode in moments like this what it wants to show you.[2] This exercise can be extremely powerful because instead of fighting, fleeing, or freezing, you remain present. You choose to listen to yourself. You take time to understand the concerns you're experiencing, so that you can factor them in when deciding on your next steps.

When you're responsible for leading the change in your organization, you'll see other people go through their own versions of resistance.

- In fight mode, people might feel like they've lost control of a situation and go so far as to sabotage your efforts.

- In flight mode, people might adopt a wait-and-see approach and choose not to participate.

- In freeze mode, people might be slow to act and feel disengaged in the process of change.

The best thing you can do in these situations is communicate. People are often more receptive than we think they are and more likely to embrace change when they feel their opinion is valued. If you lead a team, think about how the members might respond if you present the change to them in detail and ask for their opinion. Show them the cost-benefit analysis and what it could save them and your organization in the long run. Let them know their well-being not only matters but is a top priority. Tell them you're open to their insights and ideas during the entire process, and then make sure you're ready to take action in response. You can use the same approach if you're working with customers.

Willingness to implement change comes first, but implementation presents its own set of challenges. I'm sure you've noticed how implementing solutions to problems at work ends up feeling far more difficult than it should. You might be tempted not to touch certain issues with a ten-foot pole, especially if you already have other, more compelling responsibilities. Not doing anything is the easiest solution, that's true. Change requires energy, time, and resources. That said, when you add up the small issues you've been ignoring for a year, five years, or ten, you could be talking about hundreds of thousands of dollars lost in labor, productivity, or business—all because you lacked the desire to take action and implement the changes that were needed when you had the chance.

When you add up the small issues you've been ignoring for a year, five years, or ten, you could be talking about hundreds of thousands of dollars lost in labor, productivity, or business.

3. Build the Stamina Needed to Persist

One of the reasons people are so resistant to change is that the process can be drawn out, like a long and tedious race. Real change at work takes time—not just a week or two—in the same way a new habit takes months to establish. You wouldn't get up and run a marathon without first building your stamina. In the same way, you must show up to work prepared to take the actions necessary for change to take root.

I often see organizational leaders engage their employees in listening sessions or focus groups. They gather as much input as they can before changing anything, which is great. The problem is, simply eliciting people's opinions about a change initiative won't necessarily correlate to lasting impact. Once you've taken action, my advice is always to involve others by asking questions like "What would be helpful to you in terms of next steps?" That will enable you to determine how to act based upon what they need as a priority to keep going.

I recall an interaction I had with an executive team as I presented their annual employee engagement survey findings and recommended changes to them in their boardroom. The chief administration officer asked whether any of the changes that the culture team had implemented the previous quarter from the previous survey results would positively impact their engagement scores and status on a top workplace award list that next quarter. Luckily, another senior member in the room interrupted and said, "This is not a short-term or one-and-done approach. We have to stick to this listening thing we are doing, and over time we will see positive changes." I further explained that a true commitment to the change they were seeking required the stamina and patience to consistently practice and act. Then, and only then, would they see the real impacts of the changes they made in their active listening processes.

Now that you know the three steps to sustainable change, I urge you to move forward carefully and meticulously. Pay attention to the details of each step. Don't betray someone's trust by hearing them out and then doing nothing when they expect you to do something.

You must have faith in your ability to not only take action but also overcome any obstacles in your path.

I believe in you and your organization's ability to achieve sustainable change, but do you? You must have faith in your ability to not only take action but also overcome any obstacles in your path.

The Role of Compassion

No discussion about taking action would be complete without also talking about compassion. Compassion is about more than the emotion of empathy—it means going out of your way to help someone else. I've always valued empathetic listening, but compassion is that additional step that tells someone, "Hey, I've got your back."

During the COVID-19 pandemic, and the civil unrest that followed the killing of George Floyd and others, so many things changed for me—not least of which was the courage I found to use my voice and share my personal perspective as a Black woman in America. Before this global trauma, I hid my story, its impact on me, and my undeniable inclusion in a marginalized group, along with the pain that I experienced as a result. Instead of using my story to uplift and unify others, I tucked it out of sight, worried how people might respond. This trauma was a wake-up call for me, and I'm much more transparent about my journey today. I have the confidence to pull back the curtain and reveal more of myself and my personal ups and downs. I speak up on more controversial issues if I feel it's in defense of something I believe in or will help someone else. I'm not afraid to advocate for myself and others, and I feel more like myself as a result. My compassion for my community moved me, and by sharing my story, I get to inspire other people into compassionate action in turn.

As you think about how you show up for people at work—whether that be a customer, a patient, a coworker, a vendor, or someone else—are you prepared to act with more compassion? I ask this because you might feel tired, and rightly so. In recent years, we've seen chronic stress become the norm and mental health deteriorate. I have to admit, there have been times in the last couple of years when I've felt more exhausted than I ever have in my entire life!

You might also be suffering from the phenomenon known as *compassion fatigue*, which resembles post-traumatic stress disorder and most often affects people who are consistently dedicated to helping others at the expense of themselves. "Sometimes when you hear the word 'numb,' you think of a void, an absence of feelings, or even the inability to feel," said Tarana Burke, the founder of the Me Too movement, when she spoke about how she felt helping countless survivors of sexual violence in her community. "But that's not always true . . . [Numbness] can come from the tears that are locked behind your eyes that you won't give yourself permission to cry."[3]

To be compassionate, we must be strong, but it's true that our strength can waver. If you're wondering how much compassion is enough, my guess is that it's time to extend some compassion toward *yourself.* Consider what you need to feel more like yourself, so you're reenergized and ready to help others once more.

Compassion can show up in unexpected ways, and it doesn't always require as much of us as we think. There are times when people come to us to share something, perhaps after an interaction they had, and all they want is for us to *listen to them.* They just want to be heard. In these instances, if we take any action outside of this expectation to listen only, we might offend the other person.

The point is, we shouldn't assume that people want us to say or do *anything.* How do we avoid overstepping the mark? We ask people what they expect from us at the beginning and end of the conversation. In a sense, we ask them for permission to take any step past the step of seeking to understand in the Cycle of Active Listening. By asking for permission in this way, we demonstrate that we respect their voice and the opinion they have entrusted us with, and show them a high level of respect.

Barriers to Action

Besides the fear of overstepping in the action we take as a way of listening to someone, there are other barriers that many at work see to taking any form of action on behalf of another.

When I think of the word *barrier,* I visualize a wall that I must climb over, break through, or find a way around. As in anything, we can all choose to see the wall as something that can stop us from taking the next step, or when we see that wall, we can get excited about all the ways to scale it. Here are some common things that many of us see as a wall, of sorts, in our ability to take action after listening to someone and despite their obvious need for us to help them.

Fear That Others Will Say No

At a recent speaking event, I asked the audience to identify some barriers that habitually prevented them from taking action. Multiple people admitted they were afraid their manager would say no to their requests. I wasn't surprised to hear that, especially when I considered the power dynamics often at play at work. Many people feel like things are happening to them and not with them. This means, if you're someone with any kind of authority at work, you have the ability to reduce this fear by seeking out other people's input on ways your organization can improve and then acting on those ideas. When you do this, you help others feel safe to bring their ideas to you.

If you're not someone with authority, you still have influence over how others might receive your suggestions. Here are two tips to help you do this effectively:

1. Present your idea to act in the language of the receiver. Provide data to anyone who's more data driven, or tell stories to someone who you know responds better to them. Speak in the other person's language, so that they can better receive the information. If you're not clear on how best to do this, take a DiSC® communication and behavioral style assessment, which will guide you to uncover the communication preferences of others.

2. Find out what success looks like for the other person—or people— to whom you need to present your idea. What are they tracking? Is there a way you can tie the action you think the organization should take to the goals they are already working toward? If you can do it successfully, this is a great way to gain buy-in for your idea and inspire people to action.

While others' responses to your request may determine whether your desired action will move forward or not, you do have the ability to influence the answer depending on the numbered tips mentioned.

I also want to underline the fact that this book is a call to action for *you* to change the way you listen to others. You will be much less frustrated if you focus on what you can control versus how others are not meeting your listening needs. Change how you interact with others first, and you might just influence others to do the same!

Lack of Time or Resources

Another common concern for many who want to act, but delay taking action, is a lack of time or resources. I can see how this is a concern, and at the same time I often find that we invent limitations, or more walls, in our heads without researching whether the limitations are real. We make assumptions, and we already know how dangerous making those can be.

If the suggested action costs too much to implement, are there alternative ways to get the same result? Will what you want to act upon for the sake of another have a significant impact on more than one department, one customer, or the organization as a whole—and therefore does it justify the investment?

If you can include more people to discuss possible courses of action, so much the better. That way, you can land on the best solution in collaboration with others. In doing so, you can increase the chances that the change you're seeking comes to fruition.

People Don't See the Problem

Often, the action we're looking to take is tied to a problem that only a few can see. Some people live in denial of an issue—perhaps because they are frozen by the idea of change or are afraid of what it might mean for them. Some don't see—or *want* to see—the negative impact of a problem, and so they never accept that there is a need for a fix.

Again, the best thing we can do in these situations is communicate in a way that people can understand and absorb. Listen first, and *then* explain. Answer questions, and bring people on the journey with you. Make them feel a part of what's about to happen, because they are! After that, close the loop by staying in communication with them at every step along the way.

Communication is a vital part of the Cycle of Active Listening, and it never stops—no matter what phase of the cycle we find ourselves in. We'll discuss this some more in the next chapter, on closing the loop.

You must have faith in your ability to not only take action but also overcome any obstacles in your path.

Act **REFLECTIVE PRACTICE**

Your Way of Demonstrating Compassionate Action

Do you recall a time when you were presented with feedback, whether from a customer, a coworker, or a manager, and struggled to take action? What were the barriers preventing you from acting in a timely way? What was the outcome?

Write down what the outcome was and what you think would have been different if you had taken action.

Reflecting back, what did you learn from that situation, and how could active listening have helped you?

_____

_____

_____

_____

_____

_____

_____

_____

Act in a **VIRTUAL WORLD**

Taking action in a virtual world means recognizing the need for change, cultivating a real desire for that change, and then building the stamina you need to persist with that change.

Below are some strategies to help you act compassionately, even when you're behind a screen most or even some of the time:

1. Since we can't necessarily walk into the office to plan around a boardroom table, it's even more important to have everyone come with a plan they can share. Remain flexible, and keep focusing on how the action will serve others.

2. Be sure to fit in a debrief call with all parties involved to ensure that the action you decided on benefited those you intended to benefit. Ask for lots of feedback, and be prepared to learn from your mistakes.

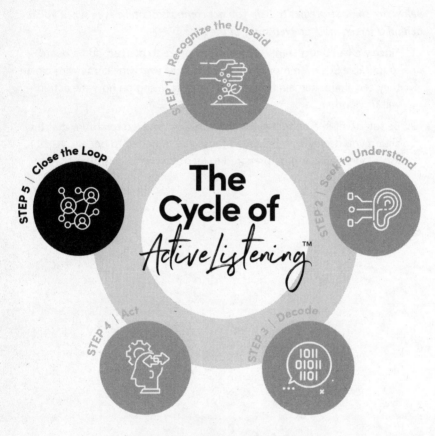

The Cycle of *Active Listening*™

STEP 1 | Recognize the Unsaid
STEP 2 | Seek to Understand
STEP 3 | Decode
STEP 4 | Act
STEP 5 | Close the Loop

Cycle of Active Listening Model: Step 5

5

CLOSE THE LOOP

● ● ●

The single biggest problem in communication
is the illusion that it has taken place.
—George Bernard Shaw

The fifth step in the five-step process we follow if we want to listen effectively and positively engage those around us is to close the loop. Closing the loop is the connecting piece (see figure 6). It's easy for us to forget because it requires intentional effort.

Often, I see people following the first four steps—recognizing the unsaid, seeking to understand, decoding, and then taking action—and then everything grinds to a halt. In contrast, closing the loop says one of the following:

- "I acted. Thank you for your feedback, and here's what I did about it."

- "I can't do anything about what you brought to my attention now, but I might be able to do something later."

- "I can't do anything about X, but I can do Y."

The same goes for customers. You can say, "We heard what you had to say, and here's what we're going to do about it," or "We heard what you had to say, and here's the end result. Thank you so much for the feedback."

You go back to the person who gave you the feedback—whether in a survey or in a one-on-one interaction or group meeting—and let

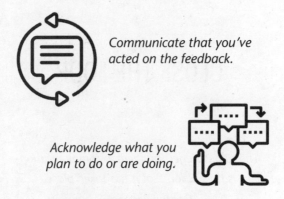

Communicate that you've acted on the feedback.

Acknowledge what you plan to do or are doing.

Figure 6. Steps to Close the Loop

them know, "Thank you for your feedback. By the way, we heard you and here's what's next."

When you validate the other person in this way, they infer, "I'm important to them. They respect my time. They respect my voice. They respect me, as a human. My feedback meant something to them."

Closing the loop means you're communicating that you are planning to act on the input you received, are in the process of acting on that input, or already have acted. A little gratitude here goes a long way. When you genuinely thank someone for their input, they feel your appreciation and are likely to feel more connected to you as a result.

This step completes the Cycle of Active Listening, but then the cycle starts all over again. Yes, you read that correctly. To be known as a great active listener, you have to be committed to doing it well, with everyone you encounter, and demonstrate your listening skills often. This is not a one-and-done proposition but something that should be an ongoing part of all your interactions. You simply keep working the steps.

Don't Just Check the Box

When I'm leading workshops, participants often ask me two questions when exploring how they might apply the Cycle of Active Listening: One, which step is the most problematic for most people to do consistently? And two, which steps have the biggest impact?

To answer the first question, I must say that the last two steps (taking action and closing the loop) are the hardest for many at work because people don't realize that listening to someone requires any action at all and that following up with those who have given feedback is like the period at the end of a sentence. It completes the active listening process.

You see, many of us tend to be check-the-box people. We think the effort toward something, without full commitment, should be good enough. I see this in the work done by the team at my consulting and training firm too. An organization's leaders might say, "We need to show our commitment to diversity, so let's set up an unconscious-bias class for our leaders." Or a sales representative might say, "XYZ customer thinks we can't handle their business because of our size. So, let's make sure we throw in an extra layer of services to win them over." Or a manager might say, "Sally expressed that she doesn't feel included in our team, so let's make sure to invite her to any out-of-work events we throw." Our check-the-box thinking causes us to mistakenly assume there is one quick-and-simple solution to solve a particular workplace challenge. But the answer is rarely quick and simple.

I recall speaking to my friend Kim. When I asked how things were going for her, she seemed angry and disappointed. She was working for a nonprofit and focusing on serving an underserved population. Kim had been assigned a large caseload, and every time she looked to review what the status was on her cases, she found the process cumbersome and repetitive. Deep down, she knew how things needed to change. On several occasions, she had requested that the organization come up with an easier process, but nothing materialized. Then, through the grapevine, she discovered there was *already* a spreadsheet that was being distributed via email each week, one that alleviated a lot of the challenges she had been facing. Since she had begun working in this position, Kim had never once been included in the distribution of this spreadsheet. Upon her discovery, she was even more frustrated and asked the leadership why she hadn't ever been included in the email chain. Not only did they not apologize for leaving Kim out, but they *continued* to exclude her and then expressed anger when she again brought up the gap in communication. After reaching her limit of frustration, Kim left that company to find a more inclusive and supportive place to work. She expressed feeling completely unheard, discounted, and undervalued throughout the entire experience.

Unhappy Lane Hospital and Frustrated Fiona from earlier in this book were frustrated for a while before we even noticed the signs. After I held a meeting with them to learn what was going on, I went back to my company and met with people internally to research our potential options. Armed with a plan of action, I was able to close the loop by reporting back to Fiona what my organization could do to minimize her frustrations. I went on to document a new process and make sure everyone understood their role in bringing that process to life.

Can you see that closing the loop requires a commitment to ensure that whomever you're listening to knows you take their voice seriously?

How to Close the Loop with Different People

How does this relate to you? How can you close the loop with the people you work with, specifically? Here, I've included scenarios that cover the majority of the stakeholders in the workplace. I want to show you how easy it is in *any* environment.

1. Manager to Team Member

As a manager, closing the loop with team members is critical to building the trust necessary to maintain a positive team culture. When we close the loop by communicating with team members after they have provided feedback, they feel like partners on the journey instead of victims of one-sided decisions. If you're a manager, here's how you can close the loop, featuring a real-life scenario.

Team member Joe asks you in your weekly one-on-one meeting whether he can have the week of Christmas off from work. In order to follow the Cycle of Active Listening and clarify his request, you confirm the dates and ask if he will have coverage in place for his shifts. You pay close attention to his body language and the tone of his voice, as well as his facial expressions, during this exchange. Then, you let him know you'll need to take a day or two to look at the schedule to make sure his request doesn't overlap with other time-off requests. After reviewing all other requests, you see there is no conflict. So, you decide to honor Joe's request. To close the loop with Joe, you don't just approve that time off in the system; you also either email him or let him know of your decision in your next weekly meeting. That's it. You just followed the Cycle of Active Listening. See how easy that was?

2. Sales or Customer Service to Prospect or Customer

Having been in both sales and customer experience, I know there are a plethora of opportunities to mess up the active listening process, especially when it comes to closing the loop. If we want our customers, clients, or prospects to know we've heard them and are trying our best to meet their requests, we must follow the entire process and end with closing the loop. Here are a couple of examples of what this can sound like.

Let's assume you're speaking to a sales prospect called Eager Julie, and she asks you whether you're able to add on a certain service for half the price. Now, you know you cannot discount that much without your manager's approval. So, you can't provide her with an affirmative response until you get your manager's buy-in. Here's how the exchange might go:

> **You:** "Julie, I can tell you're eager to work with us, and I want to make this work for you. The only thing is, I'm unable to go that low without first speaking to my manager. Do you mind if I get back to you by the same time tomorrow with what we're able to do for you?"
>
> **Eager Julie:** "Sure—I hope we can make this work."

Next, you set a time to chat with your manager and visit him in his office to see if this lower price is possible—and what, if anything, you can do to meet Eager Julie in the middle. If you need to do any other research or speak to anyone else to make sure you've covered all your bases, you do that too. Once you know what type of action you can take to meet Eager Julie's request, you go back to her with something like the following:

> **You:** "Julie, thank you so much for your patience while I spoke to my manager and one other team member regarding your request that we include another service at half the price. My manager asked me to check with the logistics team on the additional costs before he could let me know whether we could go that low. After I checked with logistics, I discovered that there would be one more cost I was not aware of that would make it hard for us to go down by 50 percent. After sharing this information with my manager, he did say we could swing a 35 percent discount off the original price for that add-on. Would that be acceptable to you as a symbol of our desire to partner with you long term?"

> **Eager Julie:** "Thank you so much for doing all this work to find a price we could live with and getting back to me when you promised you would. I really appreciate it. Yes, we will take the 35 percent discount. We are excited to work with you and XYZ company for all our needs."

Can you see how following the process worked in this example? Conversely, can you see how getting back to Eager Julie a day later than you promised and demonstrating little effort to decode, act, and then close the loop would have left her feeling? Because you took the time to listen to her, clarifying her exact needs in the front end of the sales process, and then did all the necessary things to complete the Cycle of Active Listening, you landed a customer for life!

3. Coworker to Coworker

One of the main reasons why employees stay in their jobs is because they want to stay with their coworkers. They often see them as friends, even family. You can see, then, how learning to actively listen to each other at work has an even deeper impact than we think. Whether in a physical office or on a Zoom screen, I'll bet you spend hours per week interacting with coworkers in a variety of ways. Each interaction gives you the opportunity to let the people you work with know that you value and understand them. Here's one way you might close the loop with your coworkers.

Let's assume you have a coworker named Alicia who you notice is going through some challenges. Her energy has been low, her zest to come to work seems depleted, and her overall mindset appears to have shifted to less positive. Because you're concerned about Alicia, you offer to take her to lunch to catch up. She accepts, and once you're there, you seek to understand what's happening in her life. When she tells you, you ask how you can help. You then go a step further and brainstorm with her some ways to overcome where she's at. Since you already asked Alicia if you could recommend your therapist to her, and she said yes, you take action by contacting your therapist to be sure she has availability and then make a formal introduction to Alicia. A few weeks later, you close the loop with Alicia to see how everything is going with the new therapist and also to see how she is doing overall. Alicia confides that she's feeling much better and appreciates all your support.

First, let me say, good for you for noticing! Many at work don't even notice signs of discontent in their coworkers, and even fewer try to lean in with compassionate action to do anything about it. Many would give the recommendation and then leave it at that, but by closing the loop with Alicia to be sure she was in a better place, you showed her that you care for her and value her as a coworker. Can you see how this would make her feel heard and want to stay on the team?

Now, this was a onetime example. Workplace relationships require a lot of effort. When you listen to coworkers, follow the Cycle of Active Listening, and you'll make a difference at work in ways you didn't anticipate.

4. Organization to All Employees

I've never seen an organization that gets closing the loop right on a consistent basis. I don't think it's intentional but rather a symptom of the bigger problems of burnout, overwhelm, and too much focus on getting tasks done and initiatives completed over things like listening well. As organizations are struggling with employee turnover, low morale, and low engagement, active listening is the way to get to the truth of what employees want and need to make a decision to stay and contribute. Here's an example of closing the loop at the organizational level to all employees.

Let's assume you administered an employee engagement survey because you sensed there were changes in the culture that weren't all positive by *recognizing the unsaid*. Your leadership team knew you needed to know more. The survey closes. Now, what do you do? Well, first and foremost, you have to close the loop for your employees who completed the survey and thank them for doing so. Right after the survey closes, send out an email thanking them for using their voices to make your culture better, and let them know when they can expect to hear from you next about what you discover. Then, within a few weeks, reach out to them again with what you found and some of the things your leadership team plans on addressing—and when. Then, along the way, as you take certain actions, continue to let them know that those actions are connected to their feedback.

This is the kind of communication that's required to let employees know executive leaders care about them, hear them, value them, and understand their experience. The majority of organizations get this wrong. As a result, they lose a huge opportunity to solidify relationships with their best people. If you're a senior leader and can do one new thing after reading this book, be sure to close the loop often.

5. Organization to Customers

Closing the loop with customers makes good business sense. Customers buy our products and services and give us the opportunity to be in business in the first place. Despite this, many organizations have a long way to go when it comes to letting customers know how important their voices are. Closing the loop can close the gap on this disconnect. If you're an executive leader and want your organization to close the loop with customers more consistently, here's how you do it.

As my example on how to close the loop from organizations to employees lays out, the same process applies, but now you're following up with external customers instead of internal customers (employees). The only difference is how easily you can communicate with customers, but if your organization already has multiple ways to reach them, be sure to communicate before and after any survey in the same ways that I detailed for employees.

I can tell you that closing the loop will act as the biggest differentiator you will have over your competitors. Normally, organizations put out surveys or do users' councils, get feedback, and might even take action, but they almost never go back to their customers to thank them for their feedback and inform them of the action they will take. This is a missed opportunity to prove that your organization is there to serve.

Going back to Receptive Katherine at Unaware Bank from the previous chapters, when I first approached her with the need to listen in a more effective way with the data they already had, she was curious and immediately decided to let my consulting firm guide her in creating a culture of listening at Unaware Bank. They decoded all that they learned in the process, created multiple engagement councils and internal culture teams to work through the necessary action steps, and then adopted consistent close-the-loop practices to ensure that everyone understood that they had a voice and role in the culture improvement. I can think of no better example of recognizing the need to change, developing and promoting a deep desire to change, and maintaining the stamina to see the change through than with Receptive Katherine and Unaware Bank. In fact, they have followed the Cycle of Active Listening for many years since, and I can now confidently say that Unaware Bank is now More Than Aware Bank because of its true commitment to make sure its employees feel heard, valued, and understood.

When organizations get listening to employees and customers right, it positively impacts customer loyalty, employee morale, and a company's bottom line. Embrace the entire process of active listening, and don't consider it done until you've closed the loop on all feedback.

Just like in the previous chapter on taking action, many at work see a plethora of barriers to closing the loop in the way I describe.

Barriers to Closing the Loop

While you already know what I think of when I hear the word *barrier*, I don't want to make light of others' concerns around adopting this new way of listening, and especially closing the loop. Here I have outlined the most prevalent barriers to many.

Lack of Time

I know all too well what it's like to feel completely overwhelmed and overscheduled. Many of us don't realize that we need to close the loop, and we may struggle to find time to do so. Sometimes, it can feel impossible to think about committing to doing one more thing. Instead, I want you to think about how closing the loop can actually save you time. If you validate someone else's concern through seeking to understand, taking action, and letting them know they had a huge part in creating a specific outcome, how do you think they will feel? They will put more trust in the organization and team success.

The very act of closing the loop makes others feel a part of the change they seek, a part of something bigger. You aren't losing time by completing this step; you're gaining time because you have to do less recruiting, less selling, and less convincing. Your effort to listen more effectively attracts others to you.

Assuming Your Impact Will Be Too Small

Many of us do nothing instead of taking the risk that the action we choose is too small and won't have much of an impact. We think that if we can't take huge steps in response to someone's requests, we might as well not act at all. This is the wrong way to see the positive impact of closing the loop. Instead, know that every step you take helps others feel that their voice matters. You must start somewhere, and small steps are a manageable place to start. You can take bigger steps and make grander moves once you get moving in the right direction.

Forgetfulness

With all that we have going on in our lives, following up with someone about what we did because they made a specific request isn't always at the top of our priority lists. We're trying to do so much that sometimes we can't help but be plain forgetful. Forgetfulness is often simply a sign that we have too much on our plate, and it means we need to remember to prioritize mindfulness and being present. How often do you practice calming your mind for long enough to consider other people and what they need from you?

There are only so many times you can make the excuse that you forgot to do something before others think their issue isn't important to you. It's worth adding closing the loop to your calendar or to-do list if you want people to truly feel heard and understood.

Closing the Loop **REFLECTIVE PRACTICE**

Showing Them That You Listened

Think of a recent action you took on behalf of another following a conversation you had with them. Next, write down the ways they knew you really listened to them.

Did you close the loop? If so, how? Did you close the loop by going back to them and letting them know you had taken action on their behalf?

Reflect on times you believe you closed the loop and the results of that action. How could this become a standard practice within your team and organization?

_____

_____

_____

_____

_____

_____

_____

Close the Loop in a **VIRTUAL WORLD**

Closing the loop in the right way can be tricky, especially in a world where many of us aren't always physically present with each other. Closing the loop virtually can be quite an undertaking, and it can feel frustrating if you sense you haven't quite got it right.

Where we once could read the body language of others only in face-to-face conversations, many of us have transitioned to using platforms like Zoom or Microsoft Teams as our primary form of communication. Seeing our team members from the shoulders up has us relying on reading facial expressions, and for some, this can be an easy cover to hide behind—meaning we don't know if we've closed the loop effectively.

Like the other steps in the Cycle of Active Listening, closing the loop virtually requires a greater amount of effort.

Below are some practical tips to consider when closing the loop in a virtual world:

- A big part of closing the loop is imparting the research, reflection, and time you spent pondering the other person's input or request. This sends a message that they are valued and understood by you.

- Set up a virtual meeting time to discuss the potential action you plan on taking or what you have already done to meet their needs.

- The next best thing, if you're operating in a hybrid workplace, is to wait until the other person is in the office, so that you can communicate in person.

- Follow up your proposed action plan with an email to reiterate what you discussed and clarify next steps.

ARE YOU READY TO BECOME A BETTER ACTIVE LISTENER?

● ● ●

The journey of a thousand miles begins with a single step.
—**Lao Tzu**

We're at a difficult time in our history. We've become oblivious to the needs of others because we fail to listen. People everywhere feel help-less, ignored, and unimportant to the people they work with. This, in some ways, was heightened by the move to more remote work, but it has been its own epidemic for some time. I feel called to focus on listening at work in my consulting company because I think it is the single most important thing we can do to create more hope, a deeper sense of importance and belonging, and a desire to stay invested for the long haul.

After I spoke on the topic of listening at an event, a young lady approached me to get her copy of my last book, *The Art of Caring Leadership*, signed. While I was signing it, she said, "I've always thought of listening as a way to connect with people, but you've really elevated what listening means to me. Now, I realize I have the power to not only listen, but through listening, give others *their* power back!"

I sat there stunned, pen in hand. I didn't even realize I had commu-nicated that, but I was thrilled she had received that message and would walk away with that level of empowerment—showing up differently for her customers, coworkers, and, heck, anyone in her life as a result.

That's just it, isn't it? We give others at work their power back when we commit to listening to them in the way I outlined in this book. This is true in all areas of our lives. Those in our presence no longer feel like numbers on a spreadsheet or a means to an end—they finally feel heard, valued, and understood for who they are as people.

Not long ago, I attended an annual fundraising event for an organization with a primary mission of ministering to the homeless. This is always a powerful event, especially because those who minister to the homeless are freshmen in college. We sat at a table with a nineteen-year-old who was a new missionary and who obviously felt compelled to do the work. She confided to those at my table that she had taken her second year off from college to have these types of encounters, while her parents and friends were left confused as to why she had made this choice.

Later in the evening, the organization pulled at our heartstrings by showing us a video revealing the many faces on the streets and telling stories of brokenness, friendship, and redemption. At one point, our entire table was in tears, as one of the missionaries asked us to imagine being homeless. He asked us to imagine feeling invisible and ignored. He delicately walked us through the journey.

Another missionary told a story of a homeless gentleman who started off very distant and disengaged each time she tried to speak with him, but over time he softened. When they first met, she would see him on a street in the area where she walked most days and call out to him. Sometimes he engaged; sometimes he didn't. But after some months of her visiting him, listening, and talking with him, he would go out of his way to call out to her and engage with her when he saw her. Over time, their relationship deepened.

Often, we think people are homeless because they don't have a place to live, but there are other reasons. This missionary recounted many reasons why someone might be on the streets. This particular gentleman was a product of parents who were addicted to drugs. He was then adopted by two people who later divorced. He felt lost. He didn't have a North Star. There was no one and nowhere to go to.

What hit me hardest were the words his attending missionary used. She spoke of meeting him in his brokenness. Not trying to be there to fix him, but to let him know that she was there to listen to him and that he was seen. "By going deeper and showing my awkwardness and discomfort with engaging a new person in this strange place, I showed him how much I loved and cared for him," she said. "Our hearts change by interacting with them. We receive more than what we give."

As I said, I was in tears.

This resonated with me so much because of the work I do to help organizations and the people who work for them listen more effectively to one another and to those they serve. While in most cases our employees and customers aren't homeless like the gentleman I described, they do often feel unseen and unheard. We all do.

One of my most powerful realizations from the missionary's experience was that people often don't want us to fix or solve a problem for them. Most times, people come to us simply because they just need an ear. They long to form relationships with people interested enough to give them their undivided attention.

In a world that focuses on action, there are many cases that can't be fixed. There are many times when people don't need a solution from us. Sometimes, just hearing someone out is all we need to do. This is true as leaders of teams, as leaders of households, and as leaders in our communities. When we lean in long enough to discern what those around us at work need, then we will know what we can do next.

Where Do We Go from Here?

The first piece of advice I want to give you is to trust the process. There will be some who think of the five steps in the Cycle of Active Listening as prescriptive or difficult to master. Here's what I will say: You have to trust the process. I've used the steps over and over again with customers, team members, and colleagues. I've also witnessed times when organizations, sales representatives, customer service teams, and managers missed one, two, or even three steps in this process—and they experienced the ramifications of those missteps on their relationships at work.

You can choose to be different. You can choose to actively listen to people and help them feel more heard, more valued, and more understood than they ever have been. How do you actively listen?

1. Recognize the unsaid.

2. Seek to understand.

3. Decode.

4. Act.

5. Close the loop.

I can promise you this: If you consistently follow the cycle, you'll make those at work who are important to you feel heard and valued by you. Then, all the other goals and initiatives *you* want to pursue will fall into place *because* you listened well.

Trust in the process, and you'll also begin to listen more closely to yourself and value your own perspective. In turn, those relationships will help you feel heard, valued, and understood. You've seen by now how vital each step is and how important it is to follow them in order for best results. What if you forget a step?

Listen, we're all human. If you discover that you've missed one of the steps in the cycle, don't give yourself too much of a hard time. Learn from the misstep. Will someone feel truly heard by you if you skip a step? Well, not completely. The more steps you complete, the better.

If you realize that you've skipped something, you always have the option to retrace your steps. For example, say you forgot to close the loop with Sally; you could go back to her and see if she's still having her original issue. If so, you could say something like, "Sally, I'm so sorry. I completely forgot to do something about this." Or you could say, "Hi Sally, I just wanted to come back to you. I know I totally dropped the ball on that thing you were having a hard time with, but do you still need my help with it?"

If they do, you can assure them that you won't drop the ball again and let them know a time frame within which you'll get back to them.

Give yourself grace in the process. You can go back if you need to. We're not expecting perfection, we're hoping for progress. Will you be better off than you ever were before if you only do the first and second steps? Absolutely. Will you be even better off if you complete all the steps? Absolutely.

The Road to Accountability and Improvement

Are there other ways we can remain accountable to growing our active listening skills? Yes. At the end of this book, you'll be invited to download our "21 Days to Master the Art of Active Listening Calendar," which not only will help you stay on track to becoming a master of this new way of active listening but also will place you on our "Active Listening for Those Who Care" list. Once you are on this list, we'll invite you to take part in community forums, events, masterminds, and courses. This will give you just what you need to stay on the journey to becoming a better active listener. And don't forget to register your interest in our "Active Listening at Work" workshops by signing up for our waiting list via scanning the QR code at the back of this book.

Finally, head right over to the Video Summary resource in the "Resources" section at the back of this book. There you will get some quick tips on how to use your newfound skills to ramp up your growth in this area.

The good news is that you're not on this journey alone. We can take each step together. To master the art of active listening, you just need to commit to taking consistent daily steps to ensure that those in your presence at work don't just feel heard, but feel listened to. Only you can determine how much this remains a focus of yours, and only you can demonstrate your full commitment to empowering others and creating hope for them. Active listening is the doorway to increased belonging, loyalty, profitability, innovation, and so much more. It is the difference between thinking we understand what people want and knowing what they want.

Today, you might think of yourself as a mediocre listener, but that doesn't matter. What matters is how you show up tomorrow and thereafter for those who need you to listen to them. Imagine if everyone

Active listening is the doorway to increased belonging, loyalty, profitability, innovation, and so much more. It is the difference between thinking we understand what people want and knowing what they want.

listened this way. Imagine you're the catalyst to make this a reality. Wouldn't workplaces around the world be places that people flocked to instead of ran away from? You can be the spark. We can be the spark. My hope is that you will use your newfound knowledge to spread the good news. Go out and change your little corner of the world by demonstrating the art of active listening, and positively touch the lives of those in your presence for the better!

heatheryounger.com/theartofactivelistening

THE ART OF ACTIVE LISTENING
DISCUSSION GUIDE

• • •

I hope that reading *The Art of Active Listening* provided you with new insights into how you can evaluate the quality of your listening with the goal of ensuring that others feel heard, valued, and understood. You may have more questions that would be beneficial to explore with your professional and/or personal circles. The following discussion prompts offer an opportunity for you to examine what you'll do differently based on what you've learned about each stage in the Cycle of Active Listening.

Recognize the Unsaid

1. Why do you want to listen to others? Whom does it benefit?

2. How do you feel when you uncover inconvenient truths?

3. What could be the worst-case scenario of your not recognizing the unsaid at work?

4. How do you plan on recognizing the unsaid in the future?

5. What are some of the things to look for when recognizing the unsaid virtually?

Seek to Understand

1. When can you tell that someone is seeking to respond, rather than seeking to understand?

2. What assumptions do you often find yourself making about others at work?

3. What are some habits you want to cultivate to increase your capacity to be present with people when seeking to understand?

4. What are some questions you'll ask when seeking to understand?

5. What should you keep in mind when seeking to understand virtually?

Decode

1. What will you do to ensure that you take time to decode properly?

2. What might happen if you fail to decode?

3. What unconscious biases have influenced your assumptions in the past?

4. How might you turn decoding into a collective process?

5. What will you keep in mind when decoding virtually?

Act

1. When will you know it's time to take action on what you've heard?

2. How can you be sure to sustain any changes you make?

3. Have you ever experienced compassion fatigue? If so, when, and what did it feel like?

4. Can you identify some barriers that might keep you from taking action? Is there anything you can do to address those?

5. How do you intend to take action virtually to help others in the future?

Close the Loop

1. Have you ever missed an opportunity to close the loop in the past? What would you do differently if you had your time again?

2. Have you ever successfully closed the loop? Why were you successful?

3. Based on your role at work, can you identify some opportunities where you'll have the opportunity to close the loop in the future?

4. Is there anything that might prevent you from closing the loop? What will you do to overcome that obstacle?

5. What are some things you can try to close the loop virtually?

RESOURCES

• • •

Your active listening journey doesn't end here.

Many experts say that it takes twenty-one days to form a habit, right? We've created a twenty-one-day calendar to help you form the habit of active listening. To learn how this works, scan the QR code in the boxed figure or go to the URL to download the "21 Days to Master the Art of Active Listening Calendar."

Make Active Listening a Habit

Download the "21 Days to Master the Art of Active Listening Calendar"

Ready to start paying more attention to how you listen? When you practice active listening every day, you build trust, create stronger relationships, and ensure understanding. Commit to your goal of listening for twenty-one straight days, and it will become a habit. Continue with that habit for ninety more days, and listening will become a signature part of the way you lead.

Put the active listening strategies you learn from *The Art of Active Listening* to the test with this specially designed twenty-one-day tracking calendar.

https://heatheryounger.com/artofactivelisteningresources/

Scan the QR code
to download *now*.

You can also join the "Active Listening Workshop Waitlist"—scan the QR code in the boxed figure or go to the URL and you'll be notified when the Active Listening Workshops become available.

Join the Active Listening Workshop for Teams Waitlist

Through this half-day workshop, leaders and teams uncover how to master active listening, so they are better equipped to resolve issues and improve their effectiveness at work.

Leaders and teams will develop a strategic plan of action to do the following:

- Recognize the unsaid by picking up on important signals.
- Seek to understand by stepping outside their lived experiences to uncover the perspectives of other people.
- Decode what they learn from others to bridge knowledge gaps.
- Act in a way that's inclusive of stakeholder needs.
- Close the loop by connecting the dots for others.

As a result, participants will understand how to resolve conflict, find common ground, and build trust at work for increased engagement, customer satisfaction, and inclusion and belonging.

https://heatheryounger.com/artofactivelisteningworkshop/

Scan the QR code
to download *now*.

Video Summary

Want a video summary of the three key techniques to ensure that you and your team are Active Listeners?

Check out this video as an additional resource on your journey of becoming an Active Listener. In the video I cover these three essential things:

1	**2**	**3**
A quick guide to using the five Active Listening steps in your daily life.	The #1 thing you *shouldn't* do if you want to be an Active Listener.	A simple outline of the best way to help others learn and adopt these skills too.

https://heatheryounger.com/artofactivelisteningresources/

Scan the QR code to download *now*.

NOTES

• • •

Introduction

1. *Merriam-Webster*, s.v. "listen (v.)," accessed August 12, 2022, https://www.merriam-webster.com/dictionary/listen.
2. APA Dictionary of Psychology, s.v. "active listening," accessed August 12, 2022, https://dictionary.apa.org/active-listening.

Chapter 1

1. Heather R. Younger, "Failing to Listen During the Sales Process," "The Listening Table with Heather R. Younger," YouTube, 2022, https://www.youtube.com/watch?v=jy30G3WZstA.
2. Stephen R. Covey, *The 7 Habits of Highly Effective People: Powerful Lessons in Personal Change* (New York: Simon & Schuster, 1989), 249.

Chapter 2

1. Heather R. Younger and Alex Tolbart, "Leadership with Heart," YouTube, 2022, https://www.youtube.com/watch?v=LEHnR5e2Cas.
2. Jennifer Jordan and Michael Sorell, "Why Reverse Mentoring Works and How to Do It Right," *Harvard Business Review*, October 3, 2019, https://hbr.org/2019 /10/why-reverse-mentoring-works-and-how-to-do -it-right.

Chapter 4

1. Kelsey Miller, "5 Critical Steps in the Change Management Process," Harvard Business School Online, March 19, 2020, https://online.hbs .edu/blog/post/change-management-process.
2. Greg Faxon, *Don't Let the Fear Win: How to Get Out of Your Own Way and Grow Your Business . . . Fast* (n.p.: CreateSpace Independent Publishing Platform, 2016).

3. Tarana Burke, "Me Too Is a Movement, Not a Moment," TEDWomen, 2018, https://www.ted.com/talks/tarana_burke_me_too_is_a_ movement_not_a_ moment?language=en.

FURTHER READING

• • •

Nancy Baym, Jonathan Larson, and Ronnie Martin, "What a Year of WFH Has Done to Our Relationships at Work," *Harvard Business Review*, March 22, 2021, https://hbr.org/2021/03/what-a-year-of-wfh-has-done-to-our-relationships-at-work.

Greg Faxon, "04: The Inner Game of Entrepreneurship with Greg Faxon," iHeart Podcasts, November 13, 2017, https://www.iheart.com/podcast/263-movement-makers-po-27905203/episode/04-the-inner-game-of-entrepreneurship-28053708/.

Annamarie Mann, "Why We Need Best Friends at Work," GallupWorkplace, January 15, 2018, https://www.gallup.com/workplace/236213 /why-need-best-friends-work.aspx.

Christopher Mirabile, "Unvarnished Feedback: The Advantages of Using a Customer Council," Seraf, n.d., accessed August 12, 2022, https://seraf-investor.com/compass/article/unvarnished-feedback-advantages-using-customer-council.

NYU Langone Health/NYU Grossman School of Medicine, "Having a Good Listener Improves Your Brain Health," *ScienceDaily*, August 16, 2021, https://www.sciencedaily.com/releases/2021/08/210816112101.htm.

Jeremy Sutton, "What Is Mindfulness? Definition + Benefits (Incl. Psychology)," PositivePsychology.com, April 9, 2019, https://positivepsychology.com/what-is-mindfulness/.

Heather R. Younger, "The Listening Table with Heather R Younger," YouTube, 2022, https://www.youtube.com/watch?v=esqhPKv5RM8.

Angela Zoss, "Monotasking for Productive Work Blocks," Duke University Libraries: Project Management, 2022, https://guides.library.duke.edu/projectmanagement/monotasking.

ACKNOWLEDGMENTS

• • •

To the Berrett-Koehler team: Steve Piersanti, thank you for your unwavering support of my voice and my work. I appreciate every piece of advice you gave me. Michael Crowley, I'm grateful for your candid guidance on this book. Ashley Ingram, Elissa Rabellino, Susan Malikowski, and team, thank you for making sure the book looked great!

Gratitude also goes to Maria Jesus Aguilo and Catherine Lengronne, for positioning my book for the international market; Jeevan Sivasubramaniam, for selecting discerning book reviewers and your hospitality during my author day; Katie Sheehan, for getting the word out about my book and promoting it in all the right places; Tryn Brown, for working hard to sell the English version of my book elsewhere.

To those who reviewed my book to allow me to polish it and make it more accessible: Deborah Nikkel and Jill Swenson, I appreciate your generosity and foresight. In many ways, you helped bring the best side of this work to life!

To the Employee Fanatix team: Thank you, Ashley Rivera, Loren Grich, and Hathaway Rabette for your perspectives on the manuscript and offering up amazing ideas along the way. A very special thank-you goes to Nikki Groom for being a partner with me on this book from the first draft to the last. You are brilliant! Your gift of truly seeking to understand me and my unique voice helped me bring this book to life!

To others who believe in me: To Stephen M. R. Covey, both my mentor from afar and someone who already feels like family, I'm so thankful that you penned the foreword for this book. It is beautifully written. I am blessed to know you.

Amy Edmonson, I know we have never met, but our work aligns so much, and I know you know that. You set the mark with your book *The Fearless Organization*, as it relates to people feeling safe enough to speak their truth at work. I'm grateful for your endorsement.

Garry Ridge, you inspire me with your way of listening to show care for people. Thank you for endorsing my book.

Phil M. Jones, you are one of a kind, and I'm thankful to call you friend. Your work around your book series *Exactly What to Say* has been monumental, and I'm honored that you endorsed this book.

Chester Elton and Adrian Gostick, you are both amazing thought leaders and human beings. I thank you for opening your heart to endorse this work. It aligns so much with your books and the work that you do.

Chris Spurvey, you are *the* master of sales, and your endorsement of my book as one you will give to all your clients going forward means the world to me. Thank you for your endorsement!

Yetta Toliver, I will never forget my virtual engagement with Xerox and working with your team globally in that way. You are a DEI professional like no other. Thank you for believing in me enough to endorse this book.

Claude Silver, we really are sisters from another mister! Leading with heart starts with listening. I'm so proud that you thought enough of this book to endorse it. Thank you.

Troy Washington, I'm grateful for our encounter at the University of Dayton and our growing friendship. Thank you for agreeing to endorse this book. I know that you know how important it is in HR leadership to actively listen.

Whitney Johnson, I know we have never met in person, but I so appreciate your openness to the concepts in this book and clearly how it aligns with your own writing, especially when it comes to what you cover in *Smart Growth*. Thank you for endorsing my book, lady!

Jennifer Brown, you have become someone I look up to. In some ways, we're on similar paths, and I truly respect your work in the diversity, equity, inclusion, and belonging space. Your knowledge runs deep, and that you thought enough of this book to endorse it says a lot. Thank you!

Morag Barrett, I adore you! You're a kind and funny lady who just keeps saying yes to me. I appreciate you for endorsing this book when you were in the middle of launching your own book, *You, Me, We.* Thank you, love!

Steve Browne, you are such a beacon of light and hope in the HR community and around the world. So proud to say I know you, and even more proud that you agreed to endorse this book. Keep rockin' it, friend. Thank you!

Kimberly Markiewicz, you are a gem. I so enjoyed my work with you and DuPont. I'm excited about our growing friendship, too. Although you had much on your plate, you took the time to read and endorse this book. That means a lot to me, and I will never forget it.

Melissa, my sweet friend, I have always respected your work on neuroscience and how work relationships impact the brain. I was honored that you decided to endorse this book so that others can access it. Thank you!

To my closest friends, Sarah Elkins, Kimberly Davis, Melissa Hughes, and Ghislaine Bruner, you all taught me the importance of listening when you listened to me over the years. Love you all!

To my family: I love you all so much, Luis, Gabriela, Sebastian, Dominic, and Matteo. Thank you for sticking with me and being patient while I wrote this book. Thanks, Gabriela, for not allowing me to rest on my laurels from the first book *or* the second book. It wasn't an easy road, but I hope you think it's worth it. You are my everything.

Mom, you were and still are a wonderful role model as it relates to listening well. Thank you for listening to me so that I could grow to see the importance of doing that for others. Dad, I will never forget your way of listening to me while we watched Westerns when I was a kid. You had your way of getting to the bottom of something in a light-hearted way. I will miss you forever and be grateful for those lessons while we could be together.

—*Heather*

INDEX

• • •

Note that page numbers in *italics* in this index indicate figures.

A

accountability, 103–104

action decision matrix, *71*

action step in active listening
cycle, 69–80

  barriers to action, 78–80

  compassion, role of, 76–78

  discussion questions, 106–107

  sustainable change, 72–76

active listening, definitions,
types, and overview, 1–3,
44–47.
  See also Cycle of Active
  Listening model

"Active Listening at Work"
workshops, 103

"Active Listening for Those
Who Care" list, 103

"Active Listening Workshop for
Teams," 110

additional resources, 11–12,
103, 109–111

agreement/disagreement, 50–51

application exercises

  action step in active listening
  cycle, 82

closing the loop, 96

decoding messages, 66

recognizing the unsaid, 26

seeking to understand, 52

The Art of Caring Leadership
(Younger), 99

Ash, Mary Kay, 39

Ashford, Michael, 9–10

assumptions, 32–35, 63–64

attention. *See* being fully
present

B

being fully present, 39–43

Burke, Tarana, 77

C

change, sustainable, 72–76

check-the-box thinking, 86–88

closing the loop, 85–95

  barriers to, 94–95

  check-the-box thinking,
  86–88

  between coworkers, 90–91

  customer service, 89–90

  discussion questions, 107

ABOUT THE AUTHOR

• • •

Heather R. Younger is the founder and CEO of Employee Fanatix, a leading employee engagement and consulting firm. She is a highly sought-after workplace culture keynote speaker, bringing the best insights from over thirty thousand employee stories to the stage; a diversity, equity, and inclusion strategist; and the world's leading expert on listening at work.

Drawing from her personal experiences as the only child of an interfaith and interracial marriage, Heather is committed to inspiring leaders everywhere to flex their empathy muscles and master the art of active listening to ensure that every employee feels valued, heard, and supported. Her presentations are dedicated to helping leaders and organizations create supportive cultures of care by improving how they listen to and communicate with employees.

Heather is a two-time TEDx speaker, sharing universal insights with millions all over the world, and the host of *Leadership With Heart*, a podcast about how leaders can better engage and retain talent. A regular contributor to leading news outlets, she has been featured in Bloomberg Businessweek, CNN Business, *Inc.*, and *Fast Company*, to name just a few.

Heather is the author of two best-selling books: *The 7 Intuitive Laws of Employee Loyalty*, which was named one of *Forbes'* "Must Read" books for HR professionals, and *The Art of Caring Leadership*, which teaches the radical power of caring support in leadership and the workplace.

Known as The Employee Whisperer™, Heather harnesses humor, warmth, and an instant relatability to engage and uplift audiences and inspire them into action. Her presentations are dedicated to helping teams, leaders, and organizations shine by improving how they listen to, communicate with, and empower employees.

heatheryounger.com

ABOUT EMPLOYEE FANATIX

• • •

At Employee Fanatix, our purpose is simple: to equip companies and organizations with the intelligence they need to improve the quality of work life for their employees. We are guided and inspired by our vision to help leaders shine by putting people at the heart of everything they do, while empowering employees with the knowledge that their voice and ideas matter.

As a leading employee engagement, diversity and inclusion, and leadership development consulting and training firm focused on helping companies and organizations become more agile, creative, and successful, Employee Fanatix partners with in-house HR and management teams to uncover challenges and devise action plans to build trust, improve morale, and mitigate employee turnover. By using innovative and effective listening and communication strategies, we unlock critical clues that reveal the sources of ongoing problems and help leaders see those problems through a lens of opportunity.

Whether we're building a strategic plan to create a more inclusive workplace culture, delivering an effective employee communication strategy, coaching a leader to better engage and motivate their employees, or facilitating an employee focus group, everything we do is designed to uncover actionable insights that enable deep cultural improvements, increase leadership effectiveness, and drive business results.

In more than thirty thousand surveys, here's what we've seen over and over: employees will tell you exactly what they need. You just need to listen.

employeefanatix.com

Observations

Observations

Observations

_____
_____
_____
_____
_____
_____
_____
_____
_____
_____
_____
_____
_____
_____
_____
_____
_____
_____

Observations

_____

_____

_____

_____

_____

_____

_____

_____

_____

_____

_____

_____

_____

_____

_____

_____

_____

_____

_____

Observations

Dear reader,

Thank you for picking up this book and welcome to the worldwide BK community! You're joining a special group of people who have come together to create positive change in their lives, organizations, and communities.

What's BK all about?

Our mission is to connect people and ideas to create a world that works for all.

Why? Our communities, organizations, and lives get bogged down by old paradigms of self-interest, exclusion, hierarchy, and privilege. But we believe that can change. That's why we seek the leading experts on these challenges—and share their actionable ideas with you.

A welcome gift

To help you get started, we'd like to offer you a **free copy** of one of our bestselling ebooks:

www.bkconnection.com/welcome

When you claim your **free ebook**, you'll also be subscribed to our blog.

Our freshest insights

Access the best new tools and ideas for leaders at all levels on our blog at ideas.bkconnection.com.

Sincerely,

Your friends at Berrett-Koehler